Growing Ministers Growing Churches

Reginald M. McDonough

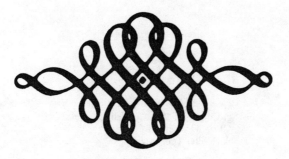

Convention Press
Nashville, Tennessee

Dewey Decimal Number 253
5290-03

Printed in the United States of America

Contents

Preface

Numerous volumes are being released regarding church growth. Many formulas are being proposed to help a church grow toward its full potential. Most of these books have some good ideas and helpful guidelines. For this we are grateful.

The purpose of this book is twofold. Part I seeks to elaborate on the statement regarding "Growing Southern Baptist Churches" that was released recently by Presidents Grady Cothen and William Tanner of the Sunday School Board and the Home Mission Board respectively. This historic and significant statement was issued as a recommendation to Southern Baptist churches and is being used by the personnel of these two agencies as a reference document for speaking and writing. The statement was developed by a team of persons from the two agencies. Although many persons participated in the development of the statement, the steering team was composed of C. B. Hogue and Gerald Palmer of the Home Mission Board and Harry Piland, Roy Edgemon, and Reginald M. McDonough of the Sunday School Board.

The statement in pamphlet form is being distributed primarily through state convention offices. It was the feeling of personnel of the Church Administration Department that an elaboration of this statement would make it even more helpful to church and denominational leaders. It must be understood that the elaboration of the statement is not an interagency document. While I have tried to be consistent with the team's discussion of the growth statement, these trusted colleagues cannot be held accountable for these interpretations.

Part II of this book relates to the second aspect of this book's purpose. Healthy church growth will not happen in a church unless the church is being led by a growing pastor and other ministers of the church. No enterprise will exceed the quality of its leadership. A church is certainly no exception.

Thus, a major thrust of this volume is to challenge ministers to give significant attention to their own growth as they seek to lead their churches to grow.

The consultants, editors, and supervisors of the Church Administration Department of the Sunday School Board have been major contributors in the development of the book. The following persons developed resource papers that have been used in the preparation of the book.

Chapter 1—Biblical Principles of Church Growth—Bruce Grubbs

Chapter 2—Characteristics of Growing Churches—Thurman Allred, Marguerite Babb, James Barry, Will Beal, Truman Brown, Bob Couch, Bruce Grubbs, Alice Magill, Fred McGehee, Marvin Myers, Bob Taylor, Charles Treadway, and Henry Webb

Chapter 3—Action Steps for Growing Churches—Brooks Faulkner

Chapter 4—Growing in Self-Understanding—Felix Montgomery

Chapter 5—Growing in Relational Skills—Jerry Brown

Chapter 6—Growing in Leadership Skills—William Halbert

Chapter 7—Growing as a Person in Christ—Ernest Mosley

A special word of thanks should also go to Wanda Harris who typed much of the manuscript and to Judi Hayes and Jane Wilson who spent many hours getting the manuscript ready for publication.

Part I
Growing Churches

Introduction to Part I

What Is Church Growth?

The pathos was evident in the eyes and voice of my friend as he shared with me the anxiety he felt during the Monday morning pastors' conferences. The meeting, meant to be a time of mutual support and sharing, was pure agony for my friend because his church was not growing numerically. The victories others were sharing only accentuated the failure he felt. No matter how hard he worked and prayed, numerical growth just wouldn't happen.

The anxiety expressed by my pastor friend is felt to some extent by all of us. We yearn to see persons saved and added to the church. This is as it should be, but tunnel vision regarding the total concept of church growth and a quickness to use the growth of sister churches and the success of peers to measure success can cause a feeling of failure that will literally paralyze our effectiveness.

It is a perfectly natural tendency for any leader to base his expectations of himself on the success of others; but while it is wise and helpful to study the leadership of others, it is important to remember that God has placed different gifts and capacities within every person. Fortunately, he only expects each of us to live up to the potential he has placed within us. We are responsi-

9

ble for the stewardship of our own gifts, not some other person's. Under the Holy Spirit's guidance, we need to concentrate on who we are, the unique mission that God has for us, and how we can accomplish that mission most effectively. Only then can we find the greatest success and the most satisfying personal fulfillment.

Tunnel vision regarding church growth is another pitfall that should be avoided. Concentrating intently on one spot and failing to see the big picture can limit effectiveness. Church growth is much more than increasing organizational involvement and adding members to the church roll. If the buggy manufacturers of yesteryear had realized they were in the transportation business, they might be our largest automobile manufacturers today. Church growth is a process of planting, watering, cultivating, harvesting, refining, and utilizing. To view church growth in its totality gives a leader the opportunity to place his resources at the right place at the right time to get the best results. A more limited view will result in shortsighted activity that might win a battle but lose the war. A discussion of the definition of church growth that will be used in the development of the book is an appropriate starting point.

An Overarching Definition

A leaflet entitled *Growing Southern Baptist Churches* defines church growth as "the divine-human process of adding to a church those who are saved through Jesus Christ, equipping them for responsible discipleship resulting in witnessing, ministering, and establishing new fellowships of believers." This statement will be the overarching definition used in the development of the remaining chapters of the book.

An Expanded Definition

Growth is a word that denotes movement. It implies that life exists and that it is the process of becoming. In Ephesians 4:12-13, Paul described the end result of growth as the "building up of the body of Christ; until we all attain to the unity of the faith, and of the knowledge of the Son of God, to a mature man, to the measure of the stature which belongs to the fulness of Christ" (NASB).[1] Later in that same chapter Paul stated, "We are to grow up in all aspects into Him, who is the head, even Christ" (v.5, NASB).

In plant life the idea is vividly portrayed. A plant begins as a seed and develops to a mature specimen of the species. Maturity is signaled when the plant produces fruit. The fruit not only offers food to the world but has within it the seed from which another plant can develop.

It is important to note that this definition describes church growth as a process of becoming or maturing. Growth is not a static condition. Growth is dynamic. The paragraphs that follow will seek to describe the various aspects of this growth process.

A Divine-Human Process

Church growth occurs when God and man work together. The church, the body of Christ, indicates this union. Christ created the church and is its head, but the church consists of persons. God uses human instrumentality to do his work. It should be noted, however, that in history human factors need not be present for growth to occur. The Holy Spirit is not limited to human factors, but he certainly chooses to use persons as a primary channel.

God acts in human experience. Christ's coming to earth as a man is the crown of God's intervention into human history. He has and will continue to act in human events. "And the Word became flesh, and dwelt among us, and we beheld His glory, glory as of the only begotten from the Father, full of grace and truth" (John 1:14, NASB). In a paper presented to the Commission on Evangelism and Missions of the Baptist World Alliance, W. O. Thomason stated the divine-human interaction succinctly in the following two principles:

1. God is always working creatively and redemptively in the course of human experience. In doing so, God reveals himself to man which affords man an opportunity for a new and progressively better response to life.
2. Men who respond favorably to God's revelation

and become obsessed with its meaning for human
life set out to share the message of God with all men
in order to convert them.²

The statements put the sequence in proper perspective.
Church growth is a divine-human process, not a human-divine
process. God begins the process and gives man an opportunity to
participate. Man has responsibility to complete the process as
God's agent in the world. "For we are labourers together with
God" (1 Cor. 3:9). "We are ambassadors for Christ, as though
God were entreating through us" (2 Cor. 5:20, NASB).

A Church Enlarging Plan

Church growth is adding to a church. When persons become Christians they become part of the body of Christ. The local expression
of the body of Christ is a church. This local congregation of
believers is the primary strategy God chose to be his agents and to
do his work in the world. As persons are added to a church, it
becomes stronger—better able to fulfill its mission. More resources are available. The fellowship of prayer support is enlarged.

Thus, church growth is not just adding persons to the universal church; it is adding these persons to a local congregation
where they can be active participants in the work of Christ in the
world. The primacy of the local congregation of believers is affirmed.

A Discipline Equipping Process

Just as a growing plant has a sprouting time, a maturing time, and
a fruit-bearing time, a Christian has initial experience, maturation, and service times. Without maturation the service potential
of a Christian will likely be limited. A church is responsible to
help new Christians mature in their faith. The new Christian may
not be aware of the goals, skills, and knowledge needed to be an
effective disciple. A growing church does not drop the new Christian once he has made his initial decision of faith. Nurture is
needed to aid in the maturation process.

Equipping the disciple is an important part of the church
growth process. Just as adding the saved to the church is an

essential first step in church growth, equipping the disciple is a necessary follow through.

In an unpublished paper entitled "Growing Christians," Roy T. Edgemon, director of the Church Training Department of the Sunday School Board, stated vividly the tragedy of nongrowth: "Growth failures have regularly robbed the church of the power and resources needed to penetrate the world with the gospel. Moral midgets and spiritual dwarfs have also accounted for much of the church's inner frictions and disorders. The poorly grounded church member, devoid of a confident faith, falls victim to doctrinal heresies."

An Outward Journey of Witness and Ministry

Several years ago Elizabeth O'Connor, a well-known Christian author, made popular the terms *inward journey* and *outward journey* to describe the pilgrimage of a Christian. The Christian life is not complete unless the inward journey of personal spiritual growth results in an outward journey of witness and ministry.

God gives persons an opportunity to respond to his call and to be colaborers in sharing his message. Thus persons use their gifts to move beyond themselves and their needs to meet the needs of others. The desire of every Christian should be to grow to the full stature of Christ (see Eph. 4:13).

The process of church growth continues to move toward completion as disciples apply their gifts in significant, meaningful witness and ministry.

A Continuing Extension of the Fellowship of Believers

The definition of church growth is not complete until the process includes the establishment of new fellowships of believers. When God created the process of growth in which human and plant cells multiply by dividing, he set into motion a principle of life that operates in many spheres. A church is a fellowship of believers. A dynamic fellowship is needed to give strength and nurture to the individual member of the body. As persons are added to a church, it gains strength. As the Holy Spirit leads, the body is able to allocate some of its resources to begin a new fellowship of believers. This is the final step in the process of church growth—a new body of believers that can initiate the process of church growth in new locations and new cultural settings.

This definition of church growth presents a beautiful picture of the strategy of God at work—God and persons working together to lead persons to faith, helping them grow in grace and in the knowledge of Christ, equipping them for witness and ministry, and reaching out to establish new fellowships of believers. This is a wholistic view of church growth.

---

1. From the *New American Standard Bible*. Copyright © The Lockman Foundation, 1960, 1962, 1963, 1971, 1972, 1973, 1975. Used by permission. Subsequent quotations are marked NASB.
2. From *Guidelines in Church Growth*.

1

Biblical Principles of Church Growth

Churches grow as a result of an interplay of a variety of factors. Some of the factors are sociological, some organizational, and some theological. Sociological factors involve the trends and shifts of community demographics such as age and cultural breakdowns. Organizational factors involve the use of a church's leadership, physical resources, and financial resources. From a theological point of view, the focus would be on the various doctrines and theological values held by church members that would contribute to or harm growth. Certainly, these areas are closely interwoven.

The fact that church growth is a divine-human process indicates clearly that we must first deal with the fundamental or basic biblical truths that are foundational to church growth. The process of church growth certainly began in the mind of God. A study of the principles given in God's book, the Holy Bible, is foundational.

The Bible Guides Our Understanding of the Church
and Its Growth

The church cannot be understood apart from Jesus Christ. No

statement of the church and its growth is adequate apart from him. Jesus is central to the church. Every church finds its life established, sustained, and expanded through faith in him. Repeatedly the Scripture asserts this foundational truth. Beginning with Isaiah 28:16, "Therefore thus saith the Lord God, Behold, I lay in Zion for a foundation a stone, a tried stone, a precious corner stone, a sure foundation: he that believeth shall not make haste," and repeatedly in Scripture—1 Peter 2:4-8; 1 Corinthians 3:10-16; Colossians 1:15-19; Ephesians 1:22; 2:20-22—Jesus is presented as central to the church. These Scriptures indicate without question: The church is built on Jesus Christ! Corollary to this is the fact that Jesus himself builds the church (see Matt. 16:18). This must be understood and affirmed as basic.

Perhaps in an even more basic way the growth of a church depends on an understanding of the Bible which introduces us to Jesus and teaches us of him. The relationship between the Bible and the church's growth and health is a direct one. Simply stated fundamental concerns of the entire church should be taking the Bible as the authority for faith and practice; preaching an orthodox, biblical theology; and seeking biblical types of growth.

The Bible as the Authority for Faith and Practice

Bill Hogue, director of the Evangelism Section of the Home Mission Board, observed that a church's growth hinges on its "ability to evaluate and apply biblical principles. Scriptural practices overshadow all other considerations. Biblical authority is the foundation on which sound church growth theology is built."[1] This means that the Bible and not some other source book, person, or belief system is seen as the basis of the church's teachings and practices. It is only as the Bible is established above other sources of guidance and wisdom that a church is brought under a common rule. "A church that rests sole authority on the pastor can hardly pry its members out of the spectator seats and make them participants in the action."[2]

The Bible alone calls all believers to a priestly role in service of Christ and man. The Bible alone contains the message about God for man. The Bible alone offers examples of relationships and patterns of living which attract men to Christ and his body, the church. The Bible alone contains the Word of God to man and reveals the Word of God among men in Jesus Christ.

An Orthodox Biblical Theology

Hogue also observed that "growing churches invariably have pastors who go to the pulpit with eloquent, positive, Bible-preaching sermons."[3] Biblical theology is to be distinguished from philosophical theology which has its roots more in speculative questioning than affirmative declarations.

Calvin Miller defined this biblical theology as orthodox, urgent, and simple.[4]

Biblical theology is orthodox or conservative. It says:

1. The Bible is the Word of God.
2. Jesus was born and lived without sin.
3. He died for the sins of man.
4. He was resurrected and ascended to heaven.
5. Men who believe in him go to heaven and miss hell.
6. He is coming again.

It reflects the basic teachings and beliefs which were "once delivered unto the saints" (Jude 3).

Biblical theology is urgent. It says today, now! It is not indifferent, conditional, or nonchalant. It reflects Jesus' urgent, immediate concern that men should perceive the kingdom of God as present rather than as coming (see Matt. 4:17). It takes seriously the command of Jesus: "And as ye go, preach, saying, The kingdom of heaven is at hand" (Matt. 10:7).

Biblical theology is simple. It is not simplistic but uncomplicated and uncluttered. It reflects a clear understanding of Jesus' message to repent and believe the gospel and to find in him new life and meaning. A simple theology focuses on a few priorities rather than projecting a great number of themes.

Studies point clearly to the fact that it is exactly those churches which teach and preach a biblical theology that grow. Dean Kelly, an official of the National Council of Churches, concluded from his study reported in *Why Conservative Churches Are Growing:* "For precisely the sectarian and theologically conservative religious groups have made amazing gains in recent years. Amid the current neglect and hostility toward organized religion in general, the conservative churches, holding to seemingly outmoded theology and making strict demands on their members, have equalled or surpassed in growth the yearly percentage increases of the nation's population."[5]

Biblical Types of Growth

Growing churches know what they want to see happen in their development, and they find that the Bible guides them in their understanding of growth. The Scriptures present four types of growth. These are not presented as either-or but as both-and types.

Growth is the increase in the total number of believers. As the Bible records the development of the early church, it reflects a picture of an ever-increasing number of persons being brought to faith and fellowship: "Then they that gladly received his word were baptized: and the same day there were added unto them about three thousand souls. . . . And the Lord added to the church daily such as should be saved" (Acts 2:41,47). "And the hand of the Lord was with them: and a great number believed, and turned unto the Lord" (Acts 11:21). "And much people was added unto the Lord" (Acts 11:24).

Growth is the increase of the discipleship and personhood of believers. The early church saw those who were saved grow in faith and commitment toward Christ and one another through the exercise of spiritual disciplines. "And they continued stedfastly in the apostles' doctrine and fellowship, and in breaking of bread, and in prayers" (Acts 2:42). This type growth was exhorted and expected in the church. "As ye have therefore received Christ Jesus the Lord, so walk ye in him: rooted and built up in him, and stablished in the faith, as ye have been taught, abounding therein with thanksgiving" (Col. 2:6-7). The maturing of persons in faith and personhood was an important type of growth. As a result of Christians' growing in Christ, unbelievers were drawn to Christ and claimed in faith.

Growth is the development of the body for effective working together. Through personal growth and the spiritual development of individual believers, the body itself becomes more able to do its work through that which every member provides. "From whom the whole body fitly joined together and compacted by that which every joint supplieth, according to the effectual working in the measure of every part, maketh increase of the body unto the edifying [building up] of itself in love" (Eph. 4:16).

Growth is the increase in the total number of congregations. Growth in Scripture meant that more groups of believers were drawn together. "Then had the churches rest throughout all Judaea and Galilee and Samaria, and were edified; and walking in the fear of the Lord, and in the comfort of the Holy Ghost, were multiplied" (Acts 9:31). "And so were the churches established in the faith, and increased in number daily" (Acts 16:5).

Thus growth in Scripture had four dimensions: numbers, commitment, effective working, and mission or expansion. Growing churches turn to the Bible to determine the criteria for growth.

God Purposes That Churches Should Grow

This biblical principle may appear as a somewhat bold assertion. Who can speak for God's intention? No one dares to do so outside the teaching of the Bible, and the Bible clearly links the growth of the church and the desire of God to call together a people who love and serve him in undisturbed fellowship. God's purpose for man was that he should be his companion; but when man sinned and disturbed this fellowship, God set about to make a new people who could participate with him in worthy fellowship.

God's purpose first found expression in the call to the nation of Israel to be his people. His acts of redemption and deliverance of Israel from bondage were an overture for renewed fellowship with man, an extension of his promise to Abraham to make from his seed a nation. "Wherefore say unto the children of Israel, I am the Lord, and I will bring you out from under the burdens of the Egyptians, and I will rid you out of their bondage, and I will redeem you with a stretched out arm, and with great judgments: and I will take you to me for a people, and I will be to you a God" (Ex. 6:6-7).

God's purpose was not limited to Israel. Rather it was

through them that he would call a new people unto himself. New Testament writers saw this calling out of a people, the gathering of an assembly, a church, to be what God was about in Jesus. "But ye are a chosen generation, a royal priesthood, an holy nation, a peculiar people; that ye should shew forth the praises of him who hath called you out of darkness into his marvellous light" (1 Pet. 2:9). "Who gave himself for us, that he might redeem us from all iniquity, and purify unto himself a peculiar people, zealous of good works" (Titus 2:14).

As the church grows through the calling of men to Christ, into community in him and into work for him, it is involved in the accomplishment of God's stated purpose. The purpose of God is indeed to bring all things as well as all people together in Christ. "That in the dispensation of the fulness of times he might gather together in one all things in Christ, both which are in heaven, and which are on earth, even in him" (Eph. 1:10).

Wendell Belew observed that "there are few thoughts of the Bible more impressive than that of God's great search for his creation; the search began with man's lostness and his right of choice between good and evil. . . . God wants him [man] back to complete that perfection which he began and he longed for the restoration of those glorious times when the two of them, God and man, could talk together in the cool of the garden's day."[6]

God desires to reconcile an estranged world, the world of man and creation, to himself. This desire is the heart of what God is about in Christ. This desire is the mission of the church. "And all things are of God, who hath reconciled us to himself by Jesus Christ, and hath given to us the ministry of reconciliation; to wit, that God was in Christ, reconciling the world unto himself, not imputing their trespasses unto them; and hath committed unto us the word of reconciliation" (2 Cor. 5:18-19).

Church growth is God's purpose insofar as it represents the calling out of a people and the reconciling of the world to God. It is not about the development of ever larger church organizations and the expansion of the church as another institution in the world. But God purposes that churches should grow and in that growth bring man and his world under his domain and into fellowship with him.

Growth Results from God and Man Working Together

Emphasis on the growth of the church has occasioned fresh consideration of a point of biblical teaching which must be resolved with each new generation of Christians. It is the question of the relationship between the activities of God and human effort regarding the task of evangelism. This point was the central issue in the controversy over the modern missions movement. The question is, Can't we trust a sovereign God to accomplish his purpose in the world? The attitude is that if God wants man to be reconciled to himself he will do what is needed. This idea undercuts the mission and growth commitment of the church. Voices within the church today have suggested that God will bring to our church those he wants to be members here.

On the other hand there are those who apparently feel that they are alone in the task of reconciling the world to God. They seem to feel the full responsibility for saving the lost. The Bible teaches neither of those extreme views. Rather it teaches that the growth of the church and the accomplishment of God's purpose through it result from the joint, mutual activity of God and man.

Paul said, "I have planted, Apollos watered; but God gave the increase." Because of this dual participation, Paul asserted, "We are labourers together with God" (1 Cor. 3:6,9). Without this dual participation a church may either passively do nothing to grow or begin to use strategies which are efficient but unworthy of the purpose of God.

"The two great factors influencing church growth are," wrote theologian Eugene Nida, "(1) the supernatural (i.e., the work of the Holy Spirit); and (2) the human. The work of God is not, however, an isolated element in church growth, but one that completely interpenetrates the basic human factors, which are primarily (a) communication, (b) economics, in the broad sense of the term, and (c) leadership. . . . One must constantly bear in mind that none of the factors affecting church growth can be fully understood apart from a recognition of the role of the Spirit."[7]

The work of God in the growth of the church is evidenced as the Spirit works in both unbelievers and believers. The Bible teaches that it is through the Holy Spirit that unbelievers are: convicted of sin and alienation from God, and given faith to believe the gospel. Jesus said, "And when he [the Spirit] is come, he will reprove the world of sin, and of righteousness, and of judgment: of sin, because they believe not on me; of righteousness, because I go to my Father, and ye see me no more; of judgment, because the prince of this world is judged" (John 16:8-11).

It is the Spirit who burns conviction into the heart of the lost person, not the condemnation of human accusation. It is the Spirit who shows the lost true goodness by revealing the nature of Jesus and God's love. It is the Spirit who warns of judgment as he teaches the emptiness of sin.

And the Spirit of God makes possible faith as he opens the hungry heart to the grace of God. Paul said: "For by grace [gift] are ye saved through faith; and that not of yourselves: it is the gift of God" (Eph. 2:8).

The ministry of the Spirit in growth is seen as he works in believers to empower for witness in the world and to bear the fruit of divine love in their lives as he gifts the body for ministry and service.

Believers are powerless without the Spirit to execute the command of Jesus to communicate the gospel and to equip disciples. Acts 1:8 indicates that bold action in witnessing comes through the ministry of the Holy Spirit. Only when he frees the believer from his natural fear of men and sets him on mission can growth occur in the church.

Believers are powerless to display the qualities of Christ's love and life until they allow the Spirit to bring forth in them the fruit of divine love. Galatians 5:20-22 says that those attitudes and behaviors which attract people to Christ through the lives of Christians come from the work of the Holy Spirit.

Believers are to render their service to God through the spiritual gifts which come through the ministry of the Holy Spirit. Romans 12:1-8 and 1 Corinthians 12:1-11 teach that Christian service is only possible as the believer receives and uses the particular gift qualities and abilities endowed by the Spirit. It is through these gifts and the ministries they make possible that the work of the church can most effectively be done. The Bible teaches that while things can be done through the strength, wisdom, and skill of man untouched by the Spirit, the result is that which does not last. The growth of the church in all its dimensions awaits the gifting of the Spirit.

Thus God's activities in the growth of the church are in both the unbeliever and the believer. Only, however, as the Spirit and man work in conjunction is growth possible.

What then is the work of man? It may be simply put that man's role is that of communicating and caring. It is the dual work of telling and showing the gospel.

We participate in the work of growth by communicating the gospel, telling. This can be by proclaiming the gospel through preaching the story of Christ—his crucifixion, resurrection, ascension, and second coming. The Scriptures give evidence that preaching is a powerful and effective means of communicating the good news of Jesus. It was in direct response to the preaching of Peter in Acts 2:14-47 and Acts 3:11-16 that the gospel was communicated and that the church grew. The apostle Paul saw preaching as the method God had chosen to communicate the story of Jesus (1 Cor. 1:18; Eph. 3:8-11).

Communication can take another form. This is the act of witnessing or giving personal testimony of the work of Jesus in one's life. Personal witness involves sharing the gospel on a person-to-person, perhaps one-to-one, basis. Each believer is, according to Scripture, to communicate the gospel through personal witness. This method is a form of saturation communication in which the gospel is taken anywhere and everywhere Christians go. Instead of the pattern of going out to witness which we have often followed in our church visitation programs, it is a matter of personal witness day by day.

Preaching and personal witnessing are not the exclusive methods of communicating the gospel, but they are the primary method seen in Scripture. Other more contemporary and creative methods are possible, but preaching and witnessing are primary and basic.

The second way Christians participate in the work of growing the church is through showing and being. The love of Christ is shown through caring for persons in Christ's name. Showing has to do with caring for the community of believers and the needs of nonbelievers. The visible gospel in the lives of believers makes the gospel believable because it is evidenced as real. In connection with this is the act of being. The Christian shows his love by being a servant in the world.

Servanthood was Jesus' way of being present among men. He taught by word and action that he meant for believers to be servants in spirit and action (see John 21:14-17; Mark 10:35-45; and 1 Pet. 5:1-5). He claimed his identity as Savior by showing the love of God in action. "The Spirit of the Lord is upon me, because he hath anointed me to preach the gospel to the poor; he hath sent me to heal the brokenhearted, to preach deliverance to the captives, and recovering of sight to the blind, to set at liberty them that are bruised, to preach the acceptable year of the Lord" (Luke 4:18-19).

Thus it is by communicating, telling and acting, doing and being that persons are involved in the work of growing the church.

A Church Is Responsible as God's Agent to Fulfill His Purpose in the World

The great purpose of God, the reconciliation of man and his world to himself, is in the hands of the church. God has made the church his agent, representative, emissary to work with him in executing his commission. This is what Paul was saying in 2 Corinthians 5:20: "Now then we are ambassadors for Christ, as though God did beseech you by us: we pray you in Christ's stead, be ye reconciled to God."

Peter's words in 1 Peter 2:9 illustrate the same intent: "But ye are a chosen generation, a royal priesthood, an holy nation, a peculiar people; that ye should shew forth the praises of him who hath called you out of darkness into his marvellous light."

Evangelist John Havlik called the church "God's only institution for accomplishing world evangelism."[8] And it is not the church universal which holds this as some abstract precept. It is rather the visible, local church which has this as a specific task in its daily life. The fact is, as theologian Hans Kung asserted, "The total Church is the Church as manifested, represented and realized in the local Churches."[9]

As God's agent the local church cannot look to the universal church, the broader church or denomination, to do what it is called of God to do, to call men to God through Christ and thereby grow. It is only as the local church does its work of evangelism and mission that growth can occur. While Southern Baptists have voluntarily banded themselves together to do what no one church can do, this free association cannot be delegated the work of each local body.

It is this local church which is gifted through individual believers for ministry. The local church has received the gifted persons for ministry and mission. And God has well and adequately gifted it for its ministry.

> But unto every one of us is given grace according to the measure of the gift of Christ. . . . And he gave some, apostles; and some, prophets; and some, evangelists; and some, pastors and teachers; for the perfecting of the saints for the work of the ministry, for the edifying of the body of Christ: till we all come in the unity of the faith, and of the knowledge of the Son of God, unto a perfect man, unto the measure of the stature of the fulness of Christ: . . . from whom the whole body fitly joined together and compacted by that which every joint supplieth, according to the effectual working in the measure of every part, maketh increase of the body unto the edifying of itself in love (Eph. 4:7,11-13,16).

God himself builds up the body, equipping it for its ministry through the Holy Spirit (see Rom. 12:3-8; 1 Cor. 12:1-11).

In the accomplishment of God's purpose, the church must take the initiative. In realizing that no other organization, group, or body has been commissioned of God for his mission, the local church must assert its efforts toward growth. As this realization breaks, the local church begins to stir to life.

"The pastor of a semi-rural Baptist church, the Pine Grove Baptist Church, Pineville, Louisiana, reported after his church nearly doubled its membership in two years, 'The greatest single step was for our church to decide that they had a job to do and say, "We must begin to grow and do something for the Lord." This was a beginning." "[10]

Bill Hogue stated: "The church, as 'a spring of living water,' has the responsibility of proclaiming God's grace; the church is God's instrument. . . . Jesus didn't give the church the role of his body on earth to see it sit in oblivion on remote street corners, or sanctimoniously grow by the exclusive process of inbreeding. He intended the church to reach out, as he had, drawing to him all the elements of society: rich, poor, black, white, brown, accepted, outcast, male, female, Jew, and Gentile."[11]

Jesus' commission to the church has within it both the actions to be taken, "teach, preach, and baptize," and the method for accomplishing the task, "Go" (Matt. 28:19-20). His examples and teachings say, "Go." "Then the master of the house being angry said to his servant, Go out quickly into the streets and lanes of the city, and bring in hither the poor, and the maimed, and the halt, and the blind. . . . And the lord said unto the servant, Go out into the highways and hedges, and compel them to come in, that my house may be filled" (Luke 14:21,23).

The action of God in redeeming man illustrates the example of initiative. God came to man! (John 1:9-14; Phil. 2:5-8).

A Church Witnesses and Ministers, Recognizing Social, Racial, and Cultural Distinctions, and Acknowledges the Power of the Gospel to Transcend Human Differences and Unite All Persons in Christ

The final growth principle from Scripture challenges the assumptions and structures of our world. The assumption is that there are natural divisions which cannot be overcome and that the structures of life must reflect those differences. In daily life this finds expression in the various ways we see people. We cluster some folks together and exclude others. The divisions include race, sex, age, economics, education, religion, and language.

The growing church operates with an awareness of these differences and may design evangelism and mission strategies in light of them. However, the church goes beyond this to proclaim the gospel as equally relevant and appropriate to every person in every group; and it sees in the gospel a new ground of commonality which unites all people. This new ground is that those who receive Christ find a common salvation and a common life and mission in him. It is not only clear that Christ came equally for all men (see John 1:7,9; 3:16) but that in Christ all men regardless of outward differences are united in him. Paul illustrated this new commonality between Jew and Gentile in Ephesians 2:14-15. He extended the unity to nullify even greater diversity. "For ye are all the children of God by faith in Christ Jesus. For as many of you as have been baptized into Christ have put on Christ. There is neither Jew nor Greek, there is neither bond nor free, there is neither male nor female: for ye are all one in Christ Jesus" (Gal. 3:26-28).

Wendell Belew observed that "new churches often find an easy beginning when established upon the common ground that persons have for their place of cultural origin or human likes. Although this may be a real asset in the beginning, it poses a later problem to the church in breaking from her cultural isolation and in having redemptive meaning in a world of great cultural diversity. The church, in order to grow, must engage in breaking down barriers, rather than creating them."[12]

The growing church may approach persons on the basis of their uniquenesses, but it must always affirm that these are superseded in Christ. In a world rigidly divided by a variety of barriers and structures, the growing church redeems and unites, reconciling men to God, to one another, and creating a new community, the kingdom of God.

1. C. B. Hogue, *I Want My Church to Grow* (Nashville: Broadman, 1977), pp. 39-40.
2. Ibid., p. 42.
3. Ibid., p. 44.
4. Calvin Miller, *A View from the Fields* (Nashville: Broadman, 1978), pp. 79-88.
5. Dean M. Kelley, *Why Conservative Churches Are Growing* (New York: Harper and Row, 1972), p. viii.
6. M. Wendell Belew, *Churches and How They Grow* (Nashville: Broadman, 1971), pp. 29-30.
7. Donald A. McGavran et al., *Church Growth and Christian Mission* (New York: Harper and Row, 1965), p. 175.
8. Hogue, p. 38.
9. Hans Kung, *The Church* (Garden City, New York: Image Books, 1976), p. 388.
10. Belew, p. 29.
11. Hogue, pp. 38-39.
12. Belew, pp. 39-40.

2
Characteristics of Growing Churches

The story is told about four blind persons who felt of an elephant and described what they thought an elephant was like. One person felt of the animal's tail and said an elephant was like a large rope. Another felt of the elephant's side and remarked that an elephant was similar to a wall. The third person felt of the elephant's leg and described an elephant as similar to a tree trunk. The fourth person felt of the elephant's trunk and announced that an elephant was like a fire hose. Which person was correct? Each person was, of course. Their opinions differed because they were able to perceive only one dimension of the animal. The point is that an adequate description could only be made when the persons explored the multiple dimensions of the elephant.

The parable of the elephant and the blind persons has an important application regarding a growing church. It is essential to explore many dimensions of a growing church to get a wholistic view. Much has been written about the "principles of church growth," or the attributes a church must possess if it is to grow. Most of the authors are correct in their assessments but risk a limitation of perspective as did the blind persons.

This chapter will likely suffer from some of the same limitations. However, in an attempt to get an adequate view of the whole, a team of Southern Baptist Convention program leaders put together the list of characteristics that forms the outline of this chapter. The team tried earnestly to make note of the common characteristics or attributes that could be observed in growing Southern Baptist churches. No attempt was made to rank these characteristics in order of their importance or to state all the unique characteristics of growing churches. The team sought to discover those characteristics that are relatively common among growing Southern Baptist churches. Also, the team acknowledged the fact that growing churches give varying degrees of priority to these characteristics.

Pastor and Staff Leaders Who Are Committed to and Involved in Growth

This growth characteristic strikes at the heart of what is a vital truth of the growth of the church. Churches do not grow by being. They are led to grow by the Holy Spirit's working through the commitments and actions of leaders. Francis Dubois, missions professor at Golden Gate Baptist Theological Seminary, California, observed in his book *How Churches Grow in an Urban World,* "From every source of understanding behind the reason for growth, one thing always emerges as significant—leadership."[1]

Richard Wash is pastor of the Cross Creek Baptist Church of Pelham, Alabama. The four-year-old congregation was begun under the joint sponsorship of the Vestavia Hills Church of Birmingham and the University Baptist Church of Shelby Association. Begun in October 1975 with four persons gathering for a home Bible study led by a US-2 worker, the congregation was provided with its pastor by combined resources from the congregation, University Church, Vestavia Hills Church, Alabama Baptists, and the Home Mission Board. By September 1979 the church had 216 members, 365 persons enrolled in Sunday School, with an average attendance of approximately 180. Its Sunday night and Wednesday night services average 100. The church has a budget of $114,000 and a new sanctuary and educational facilities. Leadership is provided by its pastor, a full-time associate pastor, and a full-time preschool worker whose salary is provided by tuition from the church's kindergarten program.

Wash credits the church's growth to the sense of "optimism and faith" which has characterized each step the congregation has taken. He leads the church to visit aggressively newcomers and visitors to worship services. A staff-led lay visitation program is conducted weekly with from twenty to twenty-five persons participating. The church conducts a ministry-oriented program with a kindergarten and a mother's day out program. Church families are served by the deacons who conduct the Deacon Family Ministry Plan. Cross Creek is the result of the growth leadership commitment of Birmingham-area Alabama Baptists and the growth vision of an experienced and competent pastor who is intentional in his desire to grow a church. Wash explains that it is his commitment to stay "from now on."

The leadership characteristic revolves around three things: leaders' commitments, leaders' involvement, and leaders' definition of growth.

Leaders who produce growth are committed to an intentional ministry. They intend to accomplish what they feel to be a priority, the growth of the church. Such leaders have the sense that of all the things that could be done some things must be done, and one of the musts is the growth of the church. Growth leadership is committed to a style of ministry that is mission or goal oriented rather than maintenance or status quo oriented. These leaders are excited by the New Testament call to be fishers of men and disenchanted by the tendency to become keepers of the aquarium.

Leaders who are effective in producing growth are themselves involved. The pastor and staff that lead a church to grow are personally involved in the church's life and ministry. Whether it is a weekly visitation program, a Sunday School or Church Training growth campaign, a stewardship emphasis, a revival or a marriage enrichment or a single adult retreat, growth leaders are involved. They participate in rather than just direct the actions of the church. They do not just develop, schedule, and delegate; they touch, feel, and experience. This involvement serves as an example which calls forth the commitment and involvement of others. Real growth leaders do not tell and sell the church programs and activities. They participate in the church's ministry.

Effective growth leaders have a clear vision or definition of growth. They are clear about what they want to happen. They know what fruit they want to produce.

Lay Persons Committed to and Involved in Growth

The term lay person refers to all the men, women, and youth who are a part of the church.

Churches in America, as well as in other parts of the world, are facing a crisis. This crisis is a coin with two sides, according to David Haney in his book *The Lord and His Laity*. On one side is "the domination of the clergy" and on the other "the abdication of the laity." There will never be enough pastors to do all the ministry of the church.[2]

In their book *Design for Church Growth*, Chaney and Lewis said, "There never has been significant growth of the church without the serious involvement of lay persons."[3] One pastor in a fast growing church said that his church experienced unusual growth when he gave up "fishing with one hook." He stated, "New Christians are being added every week because the laity is mobilized."

First Baptist Church, Paducah, Kentucky, has adopted a slogan, "Every member a minister." John Wood, the pastor, says that this slogan grew out of a changed concept of how the church reaches out to the community and the world. Members of many churches see the pastor and church staff as the only ones carrying out the outreach and ministry activities of the church. The following figure pictures this philosophy of outreach.

Through this method the church touches only a small part of the community or world. Ministry is confined to what the pastor or paid church staff can do. Many leaders and the church members become mere spectators to ministry and growth.

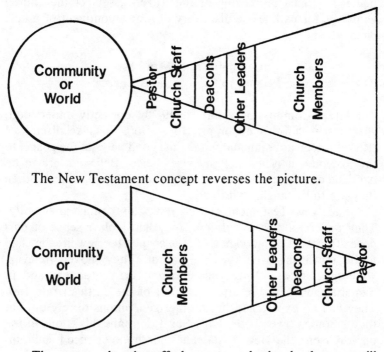

The New Testament concept reverses the picture.

The pastor, church staff, deacons, and other leaders are still in the picture. This concept doesn't lessen their responsibility for ministry. It multiplies their ministry; for in addition to ministries they perform, they become equippers as described in Ephesians 4:11-13. Their major task then becomes enlisting, equipping, and involving every member of the church, including themselves, in reaching the whole community and world.

Gibbs and Morton suggest in their book *God's Frozen People* that "the recovery of the laity means the recovery of the church." They then added: "When the members of the church in their life together know what it means to be in Christ and when they see what this life commits them to in their work in the world, they will begin to know what the church is, and so will men outside. This would be a recovery of the relevance of the gospel for the world and undoubtedly it is only by the obedience of ordinary Christian men [persons] that this recovery can be made. . . . This unfreezing of the frozen assets of the church would be for us like the discovery of a new continent or a new element."[4]

Commitment to Win Lost
Persons to Faith in Jesus Christ

The Great Commission (Matt. 28:19-20), correctly understood, specifies a church's major priority. "Go . . . make disciples" (RSV)[5] is a clear command to take the good news of the gospel to the lost, and it is listed first in sequence. Believers are to be baptized after responding in faith to Jesus Christ as Savior; then they are to be taught "all things."

The New Testament church took this command literally. They understood their mission. They had a clear sense of purpose. They told the good news of the gospel, the new life they had found in Christ, wherever they went. They moved in ever-widening circles—"in Jerusalem, and in all Judaea, and in Samaria, and unto the uttermost part of the earth" (Acts 1:8). They had no experiences from other generations to rely on, but they had the power of the Holy Spirit. Perhaps this is one of the main reasons the New Testament church experienced such unparalleled growth.

Many churches today are not experiencing growth because they have not placed their top priority on winning the lost and have not availed themselves of the power of the Holy Spirit. A church can lack many things—buildings, paid staff, and many other desirable things—but if the members are committed to witnessing and depend on the Holy Spirit for power, their church will be a growing, exciting fellowship.

The church in Acts serves as a model. It was not by accident that it became a witnessing church. These early Christians first waited for the Spirit's power. Then they received the Commission (which is ours) to cross all barriers in order to tell the good news to everyone. The second chapter of Acts tells how they were empowered and equipped. Peter's sermon and the witness of the disciples resulted in thousands of new disciples being added to the church. This growth continued and multiplied (Acts 5:14). Then the seven were chosen to minister so that others could give themselves to witnessing and preaching (Acts 6:7). Chapters 9 through 11 give the account of Saul's conversion, the spread of the church from Jerusalem, and the conversion of a Gentile. The disciples were amazed that the Word was more fruitful among the Gentiles than it had been among the Jews. The story continues in Acts of the church that put priority on winning others to faith in the Lord Jesus Christ.

Commitment to Equip New Believers and Other Members for Personal Growth, Witness, and Ministry

The Bible contains many mandates regarding the need for churches to equip all members for Christian witness and ministry. Other strong words are spoken to individual Christians for them to prepare themselves for effective ministry.

Here are some scriptural admonitions to churches and individuals regarding the responsibility for an equipping ministry:

"And He has given some men to be apostles, some to be prophets, some to be evangelists, some to be pastors and teachers, for the immediate equipment of God's people for the work of service, for the ultimate building up of the body of Christ, until we all attain to unity in faith and to perfect knowledge of the Son of God" (Eph. 4:11-13, Williams).[6]

"So you, my son, must keep renewing your strength in the spiritual blessing that comes through union with Christ Jesus. The things you learned from me before many witnesses you must commit to trustworthy men who will be competent to teach others too" (2 Tim. 2:1-2, Williams).

"Study to shew thyself approved unto God, a workman that needeth not to be ashamed, rightly dividing the word of truth" (2 Tim. 2:15).

"Finally, brothers, we instructed you how to live in order to please God, as in fact you are living. Now we ask you and urge you in the Lord Jesus to do this more and more. You know what instructions we gave you by the authority of the Lord Jesus" (1 Thess. 4:1-2, NIV).[7]

In Romans 1:11, Paul said, "For I long to see you, that I may impart unto you some spiritual gift, to the end ye may be established.'' *Established* can just as accurately be translated "equipped" in this verse.

With such imperatives ringing from the biblical revelation, it is no wonder that churches who honor these mandates will be growing and vibrant fellowships. Furthermore, individuals who take such teachings seriously will be bold witnesses and will find spiritual victories in their lives.

Not only does the Bible position the need for equipping as an action to be accomplished, but the word is also woven into the fiber of many New Testament concepts.

John Hendrix wrote:

The word equipping provides us with beautiful word pictures from the New Testament. The Greek word is *katartidzo,* from which we get the word *artisan* or a *skilled craftsman* of an art. In classical Greek, the word has a variety of meanings. William Barclay's *A New Testament Word Book* suggests the rich imagery behind the word. At times it was used for setting a limb that had been dislocated, developing certain parts of the body through exercise, or restoring a person to his rightful mind. It was also used for fully furnishing someone for a given purpose. Also, it can describe a suit of clothes which has been made and prepared for someone to wear. An army was said to be fully clothed and equipped.

To equip, meaning to restore to a complete condition, is used of restoring a thing to its former condition, as fishermen restore their nets by cleaning, mending, and folding them together. (See Matt. 4:21.)

When applied to persons, it means to correct or to mend your ways. (See 2 Cor. 13:11.)

The word can also mean simply to put into proper condition, to complete—not to a former state, but to a more perfect one to be acquired after a lapse of time. (See Heb. 13:20-21.)[8]

A beautiful word picture of equipping God's people to minister is found in Galatians. "If a man is overtaken in any trespass, you who are spiritual should restore him in a spirit of gentleness" (Gal. 6:1, RSV). The word *trespass*, literally translated, means "to fall in a ditch at the side of the road." To restore (or "equip") is to give aid to a hurt or disabled person.

The word *minister*, therefore, is closely related to the word *equip*. When God's people are being equipped to minister to the needs of wounded persons, they are directly engaged in a spiritual undertaking.

It is perhaps a fruitless debate to argue if equipping members to minister and witness causes a church to grow, or if growing churches see the need to equip members to minister and witness. Either way, the bottom line is the same. Growing churches are equipping members to minister and to witness.

Worship Including Music and Preaching That Is Dynamic, Challenging, Joyful, and Expectant

What happens in congregational worship Sunday after Sunday has a significant influence on whether a church grows. The total worship service, not just the preaching, must speak to the life needs of the people.

The need for dynamic, challenging, joyful, and expectant worship was underscored in a recent letter from a person who "has been a Southern Baptist for over fifty years." She wrote that her church is a large, traditional one that she continues to attend out of habit formed over the years. However, she said, "I find little inspiration or joy there—except in the preaching." She went on to say that the "formality, ritual structures, hackneyed announcements, and promotional 'hoopla,' along with apathetic congregational singing, have all become a source of irritation. Why should the atmosphere of our service seem like that of a morgue? It is no wonder many are nodding in their seats—victims of whiplash!"

The writer asked why we cannot have more music that appeals to the heart and the spirit. "What is wrong," she asked, "if it does bring on a few tears of repentance and some smiles of forgiveness?" She closed by expressing a wish that a spirit of excitement and joy might be a part of congregational worship in every Southern Baptist church.

Congregational worship that instills a spirit of expectancy and joy is usually found in churches that are growing.

Here are several other elements in congregational worship that are found in growing churches.

1. The worship services are led by a pastor whose commitment to the Lord is real and complete. He serves as an inspiration to all others.

2. The preaching is soundly biblical and encourages a hungering after the Word of God.

3. The services give evidence of careful planning but are flexible enough to allow for spontaneity and change. In various and subtle ways the congregation has been granted permission to follow the leadership of the Holy Spirit.

4. The spirit of fellowship that is communicated by the congregation is one of sincere love and acceptance. There are no second-class Christians. All are persons of worth.

5. The members are led to feel a part of and responsible for what is going on in the service, as well as what can happen out in the world when they leave.

6. There is an infectious commitment to reaching people for Christ and his church and in meeting the total needs of people.

7. There is an optimism concerning the activities of the church that is grounded in the promises of God. When an invitation is given, the people expect response.

Calvin Miller is pastor of the Westside Baptist Church of Omaha, Nebraska. A church located in a predominately Roman Catholic, upper-middle-class suburb, it has averaged seventy-five new members annually. This church grew in a decade from a few families to 650 in three morning worship services. In 1976 the church baptized more than one hundred members. In addition it received sixty others, mostly on statement of faith from non-Baptist backgrounds. The numeric growth registered by this church is the result of an innovative ministry in worship and outreach led by its pastor. Miller has led the church to experience worship as a dynamic, changing, and celebrative event which resists the tendency to become static.

Fellowship that Expresses Acceptance, Concern, and Love

Fellowship most often is used to translate the Greek word *koinonia*, which literally means "sharing" and is particularly important in connection with the covenant relation between God and his people. Arnold Come declared that "the central Christian insight about togetherness is this: men and creation have communion and community only as a reflection or expression of communion and community with God."[9]

It is this twofold communion which Jesus desired in his prayer for his disciples: "I gave them the same glory you gave me, so that they may be one, just as you and I are one: I in them and you in me, so that they may be completely one, in order that the world may know that you sent me and that you love them as you love me" (John 17:22-23, GNB).[10]

This intimate communion between men and God is rooted in the promise of the old covenant, "I will be with you" (Ex. 3:12, RSV), which expresses the presence of God among his people and the access to him which this implies. In the new covenant communion between God and man has been established in a new and deeper dimension through Christ's life, death, and resurrection. Man's relationship with God is now in and through Christ.

The experience of communion is not merely an individual experience but is seen in the church as the body of Christ. Fellowship that expresses acceptance of differences, concern for the needs of others, and love both for individuals and the body is best understood through the imagery of the body of Christ.

Paul expressed this imagery in his letter to the Corinthians, "For just as the body is one and has many members, and all the members of the body, though many, are one body, so it is with Christ" (1 Cor. 12:12, RSV). This concept of the church as the body of Christ implies two dimensions of the church. The first is the complete dependence of the church on Jesus Christ as the source of its life. The other dimension is the church's unity which expresses itself in interdependent help and love.

In writing to the Colossians, Paul declared that Christ "is the head of the body, the church; he is the source of the body's life" (Col. 1:18, GNB). Those who confess that Jesus is Lord are connected to Christ as a body is to the head. Without this relationship any further reference to unity within the body is meaningless. Reconciliation with God through Christ is the foundation for reconciliation among men, making unity possible.

The purpose of the unity is the building up of the whole church. Paul wrote to the Ephesians, "We must grow up in every way to Christ, who is the head. Under his control all the different parts of the body fit together. . . . So when each separate part works as it should, the whole body grows and builds itself up through love" (Eph. 4:15-16, GNB). This building up is made possible by the diversity of contributions by all the individual members. The uniqueness of the individual, therefore, is always seen in the context of the community.

The distinctive contribution of each member is made possible by the gifts of the Spirit. The fact that they are gifts emphasizes that they are not just man's talents but the product of God's grace. Paul spoke of different services to underline the focus on ministry to fellow members. He referred to actions to demonstrate that ministry is an event, not an office. He declared that the presence of the Spirit is shown through some gift in every member for the benefit of all (1 Cor. 12:4-7).

Paul went on to make clear that within the body there can be no such thing as envy or arrogance, inferiority or superiority, isolation or dominance (1 Cor. 12:15-25).

Richard Plyler is pastor of the Patterson Grove Baptist Church in King's Mountain, North Carolina. The church was begun in 1884 and continued for many years to have half-time services. Plyler became pastor of the church in 1962. At that time it was a rural congregation running approximately 140 in attendance. The membership was mostly elderly people from the rural area surrounding the meeting house which was constructed in 1889. It had an annual income of $12,000 with a missions gift of $2,000. Plyler described it as a fragmented church which had had a history of turmoil and division. It had had several pastors since the forties and the pattern of people-people and people-pastor relationship was one of brokenness and alienation.

Today the Patterson Grove Church meets in a new sanctuary built in 1967, has an attendance of approximately two hundred persons of all age levels. Its annual budget is $67,000 of which $22,000 goes for missions. Plyler described the church as having a fellowship climate like that of a family. Radical problems which rupture the fellowship are absent and "family" difficulties are resolved in love and reasonable discussion.

Fellowship that expresses acceptance, concern, and love attracts people and thus helps the church to grow. A growing church nurtures and encourages that quality of fellowship in its life and work.

Centrality of the Bible in Preaching and Study

The disciples who made up the early church did not have the written Word as they went about the business of being the church. They were possessed with the known Word, the experienced Word, the living Word.

John wrote in 1 John 1:1-3, "That which was from the beginning, which we have heard, which we have seen with our eyes, which we have looked upon, and our hands have handled, of the Word of life; (for the life was manifested, and we have seen it, and bear witness, and shew unto you that eternal life, which was with the Father, and was manifested unto us;) that which we have seen and heard declare we unto you, that ye also may have fellowship with us: and truly our fellowship is with the Father, and with his Son Jesus Christ."

This is what inspired the early church and the Christians of the first and second centuries. It was the certainty of the gospel that lighted the lives of believers and caused John to say in John 1:9, "That was the true Light, which lighteth every man that cometh into the world."

The presentation of the good news needs to be the central activity of preaching and teaching if growth is to be experienced. If in preaching or teaching proclamation fails to present the authority of the Holy Scriptures and the claims of Jesus Christ in the hearts and lives of men, it is not *kerygma*—the "pole star" of our faith.

As we look back at the past and observe the characteristics of those periods of advance for the church, it is noted that we were led by people who were "deeply immersed in biblical study and understanding."[11] It was the deep hunger for and a dedicated study of the biblical message which gave them "the inspiration and motivation for a genuine outreach for Christ."[12]

Harold L. Longenecker stated: "The greatest need in the modern pulpit is a return to Bible preaching. There has been a sad decline in the importance accorded the public exposition of the Word of God in our modern church life. Because poor preaching has almost killed the pulpit ministry, we have cast about for substitutes to fill the void and have come up with an amazing variety."[13]

To expect and experience growth when the Bible is central in both preaching and study is a valid expectation. It indoctrinates and teaches; it evangelizes the lost; and it rebukes sin and unrighteousness.[14]

North Phoenix Baptist Church, Phoenix, Arizona, is a prime example of a church which has experienced remarkable growth over a period of years. This growth has been attributed to a renewed emphasis on the centrality of the Bible in preaching and study.

Richard Jackson came to North Phoenix Baptist Church in late 1967. At that time the twenty-eight-year-old church had approximately thirteen hundred members and has grown today to over seven thousand members.[15] Jackson described his philosophy of outreach based on the ministry of the spoken word. In commenting on this rapid growth he said that "there has been a broad emphasis upon the ministry of the Word basically in three areas: proclamation, teaching, and sharing through personal witnessing."[16]

Woodland Drive Baptist Church, Visalia, California, grew from 60 in Sunday School in 1970 to an approximate attendance of 250 in 1973. Today this church has grown to a Sunday School enrollment of over 400. Growth is attributed to four factors: (1) The people have a will to work. (2) The church uses proved principles of growth. (3) The church emphasizes reaching adults. (4) A strong emphasis is placed on teaching the Bible.[17]

Just as the body requires a certain regimen for growth, so the church, an organism, needs basic essentials if it is to grow. One of these basics is the proper digestion of God's Word and its application to the life of the church and to the world in which the church exists.

Use of the Sunday School as the Major
Growth Outreach Arm of the Church

Churches that have a commitment to reach all persons for Bible study, salvation, and church membership, use the Sunday School organization to accomplish these goals.

The heart of Christianity is to show a concern toward others rather than toward self. The Sunday School is the organization which can best establish that initial contact and begin to build a relationship with needy people.

In *Reaching All Prospects for the Church* A. V. Washburn stated: "A Sunday School that is fulfilling its mission will be constantly reaching out for unreached persons in the community. With enlarged concepts, responsibilities, planning, and programing, a Sunday School can become the church's most useful instrument for reaching the church's prospects. In fact, no distinction should be made between the outreach of the Sunday School and of the church. In outreach the Sunday School will be the church expressing its basic nature in taking the gospel to others."[18]

John R. Bisagno, pastor of First Baptist Church, Houston, Texas, said: "First Baptist, Houston, is a Sunday School church. Through it we do everything that we do—ministry, teaching, proclamation, outreach, fellowship, soul-winning, visitation, and stewardship. There is no more streamlined organization in Christendom to touch the constant effectiveness of a Southern Baptist Sunday School. . . . The one-two punch of a growing, evangelistic church is exciting worship services and a committed Sunday School."[19]

In growing churches Sunday School leaders want to know where the prospects are. How many are moving into our neighborhood? Who are these people? What ages are they? What kind of prospects are they? An up-to-date prospect file is an essential resource for an evangelistic Sunday School.

Growing Sunday Schools provide Bible study and fellowship for all ages and language groups. Some are developing special types of ministries (day care, mother's day out, etc.) for changing communities.

Growing churches have growing Sunday Schools. They have recognized that the dynamic Sunday School is the best way to reach their community for Christ.

A Caring Concern for Meeting the Needs of All Persons

In *Future Shock* Alvin Toffler made a striking statement about the effect of change on persons today. He stated that persons are swept up in a "roaring current of change, a current so powerful today that it overturns institutions, shifts our values and shrivels our roots."[20] Such change subjects persons to a kind of permanent exile. They long for someone to help them find ways to cope with the forces that are trying to take their lives.

Churches exist in the midst of the hurt that plagues the contemporary world. The mission of the church is not only to lead persons to a saving knowledge of Christ, but the church is also commissioned to help persons experience the fullness of life. Jesus said, "I am come that they might have life, and that they might have it more abundantly" (John 10:10).

It is an erroneous notion that churches that are growing numerically are not involved in meeting the physical and emotional needs of persons. Wendell Belew was right on target when he insisted: "Because the church is both in the world and not of it, her being feels the excitement of dwelling on the edge of a storm. She is a refuge for her people where they may find strength but also a battlefield where war is waged for the souls of men. Without this concept the church cannot minister and may not have validity as a church."[21]

Two Rivers Baptist Church, Nashville, Tennessee, is an example of a growing church that shows caring concern for the whole needs of persons. In the decade of the seventies, this church grew from a resident membership of 908 to 3121. Marlin Seward, the church's minister of education and administration, stated that "when you reach out to people you automatically come into contact with their hurts. The lives of people are always changing. A church must help persons where they are. If you are going to minister to them spiritually, you have to show them that you care about them as total persons."

The Two Rivers Church has a variety of ministries. They have programs for the formerly married, singles, and the deaf. The church's program of recreation that is conducted largely in its activities building is considered a primary strategy for relating to persons in the community. Seward stated that about 20 percent of the church's prospects come through contacts in the recreation program.

The openhanded offering illustrates well the caring concerns that this great church has. After hearing about the hungry persons in their own county, the church voted to take an offering every Wednesday evening to aid needy families in the community. A staff member and the benevolence committee administer the fund. Through the fund the church has paid dental and utility bills and has provided food to many needy persons. The Two Rivers Church is a growing church that has caring concern for the whole person.

Caring long ago established itself as the heart of the church's mission and as such one of the absolute essentials to its existence. This thought is reinforced by biblical examples of caring (i.e., good Samaritan, Good Shepherd, Suffering Servant). Caring as basic to the church's nature is also found in the entreaty of beloved leaders: "If any one . . . sees his brother in need, yet closes his heart against him, how does God's love abide in him?" (1 John 3:17-18, RSV). The church is called "the body of Christ" and ministers in Christ's stead. When Christ was on earth, his mission was to nurture nameless masses and to cross countless domestic thresholds with compassion for the needs of young, old, rich, poor, male, female, stranger and friend alike.

Specific Plans to Grow in the Context
of Its Setting

Growing churches make specific plans because they want to meet the needs of persons. Priority planning ensures that the greatest needs are discovered and considered in the light of the Great Commission. Identified priority needs become the stack poles around which a church plans its programs of evangelism, Bible study, mission action, training; budgets; and expends its energies.

Priority planning enables a church to take the emphasis off of activity and place it on output—results. Priority planning challenges us to state in clear, measurable terms what we want to accomplish for whom, to what extent—how many or much—and by when?

Someone has said, "If you don't care where you are going, the road will take you there." Setting measurable growth goals challenges us to consider where we are going before we plan how we will get there.

God has given every church a unique objective. The church's objective is how the church will carry out God's purpose in a particular location at a given time. A study of the New Testament Scriptures such as 1 John 4:7-12; Luke 24:46-48; Acts 4:12; Hebrews 10:25; Ephesians 4:2-4; 1 Thessalonians 5:13; Galatians 6:10; and 1 John 2:3-6 will enable a church to find an answer to the question, What is God's purpose for this church?

When the First Baptist Church, Hendersonville, Tennessee, a fast-growing church near Nashville, surveyed its community at the point of felt need, it discovered that the community would grow from 24,600 (1979) to 91,500 (1990). A close study of the felt needs of these newcomers indicated that the church must not just group persons as either saved or lost, churched and unchurched, but must diversify its programs to reach out to groups of persons such as students, singles and formerly married, exceptional and handicapped children, senior citizens, single parents with children, the deaf, and youth. This church's remarkable openness to the needs of others and the ability to plan an unusual degree of diversity into its program is evidence of what can be achieved when a church makes plans to grow in the context of its community.

A World Concern Through Scriptural
Giving and Individual Participation

The Bible does not differentiate between evangelism and missions, but today we define missions as that activity away from the local church which has winning the lost as its primary purpose whether it be home missions or foreign missions. But these mission endeavors do not seem to take place until there is a missionary emphasis within a local congregation. The missionary thrust or zeal of a congregation is manifested only as members give of their money and take part in mission enterprises both at home and overseas.

The mission emphasis permeates all aspects of a growing church's life. In Sunday School teachers use every opportunity to underscore the mission message of the Bible. Mission organizations along with Church Training, the music ministry, and special events provide information about mission needs and opportunities for service beginning at home and extending around the world.

Since the organization of the Southern Baptist Convention in 1845, Southern Baptists have seen the importance of unity to extend God's kingdom. The Cooperative Program initiated in 1925 offers to churches a way to take part in many different mission ministries—educational institutions, children's homes, homes for the aging, hospitals, radio and television programs, state papers, church literature, books, home and foreign missions.

Not only does growth occur when an individual church increases its size, but growth also occurs when a church establishes new fellowships of believers.

A moving illustration of this kind of missions involvement comes from Baptist history. In 1755, Shubal Stearns and fifteen others began a church in Sandy Creek, North Carolina. The historian Morgan Edwards said: "Sandy Creek church is the mother of all the Separate Baptists. From this Zion went forth the word, and great was the company of them who published it: it, in 17 years, has spread branches westward as far as the great river Mississippi; southward as far as Georgia; eastward to the sea and Chesapeake Bay; and northward to the waters of the Potomac; it, in 17 years, is become the mother, grandmother, and great-grandmother to 42 churches, from which sprang 125 ministers.''[22]

But by 1771, because of heavy migration of Separate Baptists to Kentucky and Tennessee, the membership of Sandy Creek Church became quite small. However, historians believe Baptists would not have spread so rapidly on the frontier if it had not been for this zealous group. Even though the original church seemingly died, other churches begun by this church followed their mission example. Baptists who can trace their roots to the Sandy Creek Church number in the millions just in the United States.

Many persons today are expressing their world concern through giving money and participating individually. An example of this kind of participation can be found in the Woodmont Baptist Church in Nashville where members not only give generously of their money but also give of themselves. Missions in this church has been personalized. Many members have served as overseas mission volunteers, such as a doctor and his wife who spent a month in Nigeria, three work crews of fifteen men each who helped with reconstruction after an earthquake in Guatemala, a doctor who spent a month in Korea, a student who worked two months in the Dominican Republic, a businessman who went to Japan, and a single adult who served through the Mission Service Corps.

Several things made these people want to serve. The church provides a missionary residence for furloughing missionaries. Information is shared through an active missions committee and an alert Woman's Missionary Union. From the pulpit the congregation, along with a television audience of over sixty thousand, catches the enthusiasm for missions which the pastor and mission volunteers project. This is evident by the more than $47,000 given to the Lottie Moon Christmas offering in 1979 in addition to regular Cooperative Program giving in a church whose Sunday School averages around seven hundred. ''Traditionally, 60 percent of the church's budget overage has gone to some aspect of missions.

Last year the money was appropriated to help meet volunteers' expenses.''[23]

A Prayerful Sensitivity to the
Leadership of the Holy Spirit

The final characteristic relates to the prayerful sensitivity of growing churches to the Holy Spirit's leadership. Without exception growing churches are characterized by a deep commitment to prayer. It is through prayer that a church is able to understand its mission and to have the courage to pursue it aggressively.

After explaining the many ministries of the Two Rivers Baptist Church that were listed in an earlier section, Seward added that prayer was, in his opinion, the key to the growth and ministries. The church has prayer breakfasts three mornings each week composed of different members. A large amount of each deacons' meeting is given to prayer. The people pray believing that God will hear and answer their prayer. This testimony was echoed time and again as the leaders of growing churches were interviewed.

The relationship of prayer to church growth is reflected in three ways: (1) The life-style of persons apart from God demands intercessory prayer on their behalf. (2) The need for the power of God in the lives of Christians calls for Christians to attune their hearts to God through prayer. (3) The forces of Satan that continually influence the affairs of persons requires the church to call on the power of God to defeat the evil one.

The apostle Paul stated in Ephesians 6:12, "For we wrestle not against flesh and blood, but against principalities, against powers, against the rulers of the darkness of this world, against spiritual wickedness in high places."

Prayer brings the source of life and power, God, and the objects needing that life and power together. Growing churches are praying churches.

1. Francis M. Dubose. *How Churches Grow in an Urban World* (Nashville: Broadman, 1978), p. 169.
2. David Haney, *The Lord and His Laity* (Nashville: Broadman, 1978), pp. 22-24.
3. Charles L. Chaney and Ron S. Lewis, *Design for Church Growth* (Nashville: Broadman, 1977), pp. 172-73.
4. Mark Gibbs and T. Ralph Morton. *God's Frozen People* (Philadelphia: Westminster, 1965), p. 158.

5. From the Revised Standard Version of the Bible. copyrighted 1946. 1952. © 1971, 1973. Subsequent quotations are marked RSV.

6. From *The New Testament, a Translation in the Language of the People*, by Charles B. Williams. Copyright 1937 and 1966. Moody Press, Moody Bible Institute of Chicago. Used by permission. Subsequent quotations are marked Williams.

7. HOLY BIBLE New International Version, copyright © 1978, New York Bible Society. Used by permission.

8. John Hendrix. "Equipping: Word Pictures from the New Testament," *Church Training*, October 1979, p. 6.

9. Arnold B. Come. *Agents of Reconciliation* (Philadelphia: Westminster, 1960), pp. 41-42.

10. From the *Good News Bible*, the Bible in Today's English Version. Old Testament: Copyright © American Bible Society 1976; New Testament: Copyright © American Bible Society 1966, 1971, 1976. Used by permission. Subsequent quotations are marked GNB.

11. J. Terry Young. *The Church—Alive and Growing!* (Nashville: Broadman, 1978), p. 114.

12. Ibid.

13. Harold L. Longenecker. *Building Town and Country Churches* (Chicago: Moody, 1973), p. 88.

14. Ibid., p. 93.

15. C. B. Hogue. *I Want My Church to Grow* (Nashville: Broadman, 1977), p. 20.

16. Eugene Skelton. *Ten Fastest Growing Southern Baptist Sunday Schools* (Nashville: Broadman, 1974), p. 100.

17. Ibid., p. 15.

18. A. V. Washburn. *Reaching All Prospects for the Church* (Nashville: Convention, 1964), p. 29.

19. "Pastors Speak Out on the Sunday School," Sunday School Department, Sunday School Board, Nashville, Tennessee, 1979, p. 2 (available from state Sunday School Departments).

20. Alvin Toffler. *Future Shock* (New York: Random House, 1970), p. 1.

21. Wendell Belew. *Churches and How They Grow* (Nashville: Broadman, 1971), p. 20.

22. Robert A. Baker. *The Southern Baptist Convention and Its People 1607-1972* (Nashville, Broadman, 1974), p. 50.

23. Bill Sherman. "Keys to Missions: Motivation and Involvement," *Church Administration*, December 1979, p. 28.

3

Action Steps
for Growing Churches

A conference on church growth was conducted recently at Yreka, California, for workers in churches with a membership of not more than 150. The participants were from small churches in California, New Mexico, Oklahoma, Colorado, and Texas.

Reporting on the conference, the Louisiana Baptist newsmagazine, *Baptist Message,* released a news story which stated: "Members must believe their church can grow before it will grow was the consensus of workers from small churches." The article was entitled "Attitude Called Key in Small Church Growth."

The conclusion reached by these conferences certainly comes as no surprise. The Scripture says, "For as he thinketh in his heart, so is he" (Prov. 23:7). A person's attitude has always been a constraint on his actions.

It is also a fact that attitude is shaped by leadership. The church's attitude toward growth is directly related to the attitude and actions of the pastor, staff (if a church has full- or part-time staff members), deacons, and leaders of the church program organizations. These persons are the growth leaders of a church. The attitude of a church will not rise above the attitude of its leaders.

The leadership of the pastor is by far the most influential in developing and maintaining a growth-oriented attitude among other church leaders and church members. What type leadership style is best to achieve church growth? This is a complex question that unfortunately has no simple answer.

"W. A. Criswell . . . credits the growth of First Baptist, Dallas, largely to expository preaching of the Word. But Robert Schuller rarely preaches an expository message. His topical messages communicate 'possibility thinking' to unbelievers who know nothing about the Bible and care little whether they do."[1] Both W. A. Criswell and Robert Schuller are pastors of churches that have had phenomenal church growth in terms of statistics and buildings. On the other hand, James Kennedy "will single out house-to-house visitation as the most effective means for growth in Florida, but Stephen Olford tried it in New York City to no avail. He depends more on penetrating the high-rises through television. Richard Halverson finds that developing small koinonia groups is his best approach in Washington."[2] What has been learned from this complexity of reasons for church growth? The leadership has been not only different but in some cases diametrically opposite in terms of technique.

Leadership Qualities Needed

Several different kinds of leadership have been effective in church growth. Therefore, it is impossible to point to specific leadership qualities that are needed for church growth.

Because of the complexity, it is dangerous to establish the qualities necessary for leadership in church growth. Peter Wagner explains that different leadership techniques have worked in different churches and in different locations, but it is possible to look at some of the qualities normally found in effective growth leaders.

Wagner summarizes these qualities as follows:[3]

1. "Single-minded obedience." Leaders must be willing to pay the price for doing whatever is necessary to obey and fulfill God's direction as given in the Great Commission.

2. "Clearly defined objectives." The leader who is effective

in church growth can act with no reluctance to "set measurable goals and to allow their success or failure to be evaluated in the light of these goals, risky as this procedure might seem to some."

3. "Reliance on discerning research." Reliable research guides the leader to select the most effective projects and methods.

4. "Ruthlessness in evaluating results." The ruthlessness about which he speaks may come closer to meaning unbending tenacity to use the most effective methods.

5. "An attitude of optimism and faith." Certainly this is one quality that can be established with little argument.

A number of other competent writers have described varying kinds of effective leadership of ministers. Some popular examples are Urban T. Holmes III in *The Future Shape of Ministry*, Seward Hiltner in *Ferment in the Ministry*, and Wayne E. Oates in *The Christian Pastor*. There are dozens more. Recently Carnegie Samuel Calian summarized some more current models of ministry in his *Today's Pastor in Tomorrow's World*. He suggested that these models for ministry might include, "the servant-shepherd, the politician-prophet, the preacher-teacher, the evangelist-charismatic, the builder-promoter, the manager-enabler, the liturgist-celebrant, and the specialized ministries—e.g. chaplaincy, marriage counseling, etc."

Regardless of the style of leadership a minister chooses, the key to success will be to maximize his own gifts and to augment his style with the gifts of others. Obviously, a leader needs to understand himself and his gifts in order to adhere to this admonition. Help in this regard is included in the chapters which follow.

To maximize one's unique leadership gifts, several practical guidelines should be noted.

Avoid the either-or syndrome.—Simply stated this means that the leader who is working with church growth as the highest priority in his own leadership should be careful to help others know that church growth is a part of the Christian pilgrimage but not all of the Christian pilgrimage. For example, it is tempting for the evangelist-charismatic leader to spend so much of his energy getting persons to make decisions that he forgets the Bible study program of the church, the training program, the equipping ministry of the work of the deacons, and the missions program. Healthy church growth should not cause church members to make frequent decisions on whether they should spend their energy on bringing others into the fellowship to the exclusion of helping those who are already in the fellowship to grow in grace through an effective training program.

Interpret the whole mission of the church.—When a sixteen-year-old boy has grown to a phenomenal six feet eight inches and weighs two hundred pounds, he is in danger of experiencing the inebriation of power. He looks at others and compares. He may feel the urge to superimpose his own will on his peers. A growing church may do the same. It is possible for one church to infuriate a sister church with power. The attitude of "you don't want to go there when you can come here!" may become as natural as breathing. The leader can help avoid this feeling by interpreting the whole mission of the church. He should spend as much time interpreting the meaning of growth in grace as he does in interpreting the meaning of growth in numbers.

Be skilled in good timing.—Time will be a factor in growth. Timing will become the primary skill of the minister. He must know when the energies of growth are about to be expended. He must know that they will not last. Growth will come in spurts much as a child grows. Some months the church will grow faster than others.

The cycles of growth will invariably chart much like an electroencephalogram. It will have ragged edges. It will shoot up in unpredictable splurges. The minister then becomes a kind of counterpuncher. He will wait to see where those splurges of growth occur and try to counter with the appropriate response which utilizes those energies. Healthy growth recognizes the ragged edges, and healthy leaders are not stunned by these ragged edges whether they are shooting up or down. The skilled leader knows when as much as he knows how.

Be alert to overdependence.—The leader should be alert to the danger of overdependence. Dependence, in small doses, helps most pastors and church leaders to survive. It is a good, warm feeling to know that people depend on us. We often find ourselves baiting others to depend on us. An example may be, "Call me when you need me!" or "I'm as near as your phone!" or "Before you make any decision, please let me know."

The main source of trouble with dependence or overdependence is that it tends to shift the responsibility from the church member to the pastoral leader. The member becomes more an observer than a participant. He stands aside and watches as his church grows. He thinks, *Isn't it wonderful that our church is growing under the leadership of our pastor.* The only problem is that if the church stops growing for a period in like manner he feels, *Perhaps we need another kind of leadership since our church is not growing.* The alert leader will try to check dependence before it becomes overdependence.

Beware of corporate guilt.—Leaders who are responsible for church growth need to be alert to the problem of corporate guilt. Corporate guilt is different from individual guilt. For example, individual guilt, as it relates to the leader, deals with the one-to-one relationship of the person who follows. The church member, or follower, would react to the leader based on his own set of needs, hopes, or desires. He may feel affectionate or hostile based on whether the leadership style of the pastor meets his own particular needs.

Corporate guilt is different. Corporate guilt is the guilt which comes when one church begins to compare itself with another. Temple Avenue Baptist Church looks at Pennsylvania Avenue Baptist Church, only twelve blocks away in a city of 750,000, and corporately feels, *They are growing and we are not.* The quickest and easiest solution is to blame the leadership. In short, "Our church is guilty of not growing because we do not have effective leaders."

Pastors and church leaders who are attributed the credit for church growth during its surge also bear the brunt of the blame when church growth ceases. Someone has to be the recipient of the corporate guilt of the church. Therefore, the leaders must be significantly aware of the church's attitude toward growth if they are to carry the banner.

Set realistic criteria.—The emerging feelings of worthlessness somehow strangely get tied up with church growth. *Growth* is not spelled "worth." Some make the two synonymous.

It is important for the church leader to value growth, but he should value it in proper perspective. For example, a pastor pleads for response during the invitation period of a worship experience. In the course of his plea, he says, perhaps out of his own energy flow, "Our church cannot expect to show others the Spirit of Christ unless we are having visible decisions weekly." That kind of criteria for showing the Spirit of Christ is much like an ultimatum. What are the reactions of the church members? How do they feel when there are no public decisions? The church believed in the pastor, but he has suggested that the measurement of growth is seen in weekly decisions. In fact, the implication seemed to be that the church is not growing at all if decisions are not made weekly.

View success with a healthy outlook.—He is not enamored with the members, monies, and buildings games. He is not, however, adverse to the numbers, monies, and buildings as a by-product of a healthy, growing membership.

Is church growth dependent on personal growth, especially the personal growth of the leader? Both church growth and personal growth are processes, not events. Both personal growth and church growth have an operative risk which affects the other. Also, both have a wholistic view of discipleship.

What leadership style is best for church growth? The answer could be, It is too complex to make definite conclusions. However, these practical guidelines have been found to be helpful to pastors regardless of the specific leader style they embrace.

Actions Toward Growth

What steps can a pastor take to lead a church to grow? Certainly, pastors of growing churches use a variety of procedures. However, the following actions represent a consensus of the plans advocated by many successful pastors.

Commit yourself as pastor to the church's growth.—Share your commitment with the church that growth is at the center of the church's mission. As the primary leader of a church, the pastor's own heart commitments are shaping factors in what the church does. A pastor prayerfully committed to growth is a man on mission. He has clarity of purpose and intent of action. The pastor's vision for the church's future becomes the way he measures the church's success.

Cultivate, equip, and challenge the church's leadership teams to accept growth as a priority concern.—Involvement of the church's key leaders is absolutely necessary if the church is to attain healthy and sustained growth. Such groups as the deacons, the church council, church program organization councils (Sunday School, Church Training, Brotherhood, WMU, music), evangelism committee, missions committee, stewardship committee, are among the most vital. Such leaders and groups must be challenged and equipped to make growth a personal concern.

Know the needs and opportunities for growth.—Every church has unique needs and opportunities for growth. Discover the unreached and lost persons in the community. This kind of focus shows the opportunities for a church and should precede the design of a strategy for growth.

Establish specific growth goals.—With a vision of lost and unreached persons, a church can place high priorities on its resource for growth goals. Planning growth goals for a church must reflect a great faith and vision. It should never be done without prayer and dependence on the Holy Spirit. Through prayer, personal Bible study, and study of the church's growth opportunity, the pastor and church leaders establish challenging growth goals. Growth goals start with the question, What should your church be three, five, seven years from today?

Develop and personally direct the strategy for growth.— These essential elements should be important parts of the strategy:

- Make the biblical truths on witnessing and outreach central in preaching and teaching.
- Conduct worship services that are warm and challenging and create expectancy and hope.
- Build a fellowship climate that is warm and expresses a witnessing-outreach concern for all persons.
- Equip and motivate lay persons to be involved in the growth strategy.

- Use the Sunday School as the growth/outreach arm of the church.
- Train new believers to become involved in the growth outreach strategy of their church.
- Establish new fellowships of believers in all cultural settings.

Evaluate and continually reshape the church's growth plans.—Dynamic growth plans must continually be renewed. As methods lose their effectiveness, new ideas are needed to take their place. Plans that do not work should be discarded. Good feedback, evaluation, and redesign are needed to maintain vitality.

Celebrate the work of the Holy Spirit in the midst of his people.

1. C. Peter Wagner, *Your Church Can Grow* (Glendale, Calif.: Regal, 1971), p. 29.
2. Ibid., pp. 29-30.
3. Ibid., pp. 30-31.

Part II

Growing Ministers

Introduction to Part II

Relating Church Growth and Personal Growth

In his book *I Want My Church to Grow*, C. B. Hogue wrote: "Christ put the church in the world to be about mission. It is to communicate his message of hope for humanity's condition. This cannot be accomplished until the church members become a sharing community—a reconciled community—excited about their potential, alive to their future. Activities and organizations cannot substitute for purpose."[1] The person who is Christian in his outlook and attitude exudes his growth through a sharing community, a reconciled community. He is excited about his potential for growth in the same manner that he is excited about his understanding for the potential growth of his church.

Church growth is dependent on personal growth because both are processes.—A church that grows is not an event; it is a process. An event suggests a happening. A growth experience is a time when something happens. The reason some expectations for church growth die is church leaders plan for, hope for, and then expedite an event. For example, high attendance Sundays are not strategies to make the church grow nearly so much as they are the result of something significant going on in the church. High attendance Sundays should be the result of a church growth process. The problem arises when high attendance Sunday becomes the end instead of the means to an end, that is, church growth.

Like church growth, personal growth is a process. A person who experiences personal growth cannot calendar the event. He may point to a personal growth experience as a part of his overall growth. An example is the Personal and Professional Growth experience conducted at the Sunday School Board. The eleven-day experience has given several hundred ministers some strategic episodes of personal growth. However, the Personal and Professional Growth experience itself is a part of a process. Pre-planning goes on for eight weeks before the participant actually resides in Nashville for the eleven-day experience. Afterwards, a year is planned for activities which are a significant part of the personal growth experience. If the success or failure of the minister's personal growth is dependent on the eleven days of residence in Nashville, he is sure to be disappointed. Instead, he works the eleven-day period into the process of his personal growth which has been going on before he comes and will continue after he returns to his church and home.

Church growth is dependent on personal growth because both have interdependent energy.—Church growth is the natural habitat for personal growth. The personal growth of a minister should find expression in church growth. An example is given in Luke 24:49: "And, behold, I send the promise of my Father upon you: but tarry ye in the city of Jerusalem, until ye be endued with power from on high." Jesus expected the power to act to come from within the church itself. The disciples' personal strength would be built in the embryonic structure of the church. John Havlik explained: "Their empowering experience was an experience with the Holy Spirit that gave the vision venture (Acts 2:1-4). God doesn't want us to go in our own strength. Growing an evangelistic church is more than pastoral drive, initiative, and ambition. It is more than effective administration, good educational programs, or just meeting the needs of persons. It is the calm, quiet, but dynamic faith that we are not alone in our venture."[2] The key words in this picturesque commentary are "we are not alone." The church provides the environment within which can be found the "calm, quiet, but dynamic faith" for a venture in personal growth.

John Claypool told a brief parable in one of his weekly sermons in Jackson, Mississippi: "I love the little story of the day a medieval peasant met a monk in the road and asked, 'What do you holy men do up there in the monastry so close to God?' The monk was full both of honesty and humility, and he answered: 'What do we holy men do up in the monastry? I'll tell you. We fall down, and we get up. We fall down, and we get up. We fall down, and we get up.' ''³

That is the meaning of the interdependent energy of personal growth and church growth. If we fall down and we have not God, if we fall down and we have not each other, if we fall down and have not the energy of the church that grows, we will not grow. We will not get up. We will stay down and become depressed. We will stay down and feel the feelings of futility; we will want to quit.

On the other hand, if we fall down and have the aid of both God and man, we will get up. We will fall down, and we will get up. We have the encouragement from our Lord and from our church family to know the importance of getting up. And getting up is growing. We cannot grow until we get up. We know that we must fall because we are sinners and we are human. The energy which makes us want to get up to grow is within the church and, therefore, is within us. We will grow because of it.

Church growth is dependent on personal growth because each has an operative risk which affects the other.—At first glance, "operative risk" may seem a little farfetched, but on closer scrutiny this factor is the most profound factor of the dependence of church growth on personal growth.

When a rubber band is stretched to its fullest capacity, it runs the risk of breaking. If it breaks, it may injure someone because of the spring which comes from the tension. There is risk involved in stretching a rubber band to its fullest capacity. But have you tried to pick up a rubber band for observation without stretching it beyond its natural length? It is difficult to do. The natural instinct of handling a rubber band is to stretch it and not only to stretch it but to stretch it as far as it will go.

The commentary of the rubber band on church and personal growth is effusive. It runs in many directions. The rubber band can protect and separate, but it is flexible. Church growth can protect the individual who is growing personally because it gives the person an environment within which he can grow. It is like the rubber band in that it is flexible; it gives the individual room to grow.

It is difficult, as has been stated, to handle a rubber band without stretching it. It is also difficult to stay within the environs and workings of church growth and remain stagnant personally. When an individual is a part of the process of church growth, he is more likely to grow. He runs the risk of being stretched—often beyond capacity—but he has also the comfort of knowing he has moderately defined boundaries.

An operative risk is exciting. A child plays with rubber bands. The activity is exciting because it is unpredictable. Church growth is exciting because of the risk. When a pastor moves to a new church field, he is often heard to explain, "I wanted to go to a new challenge!" A challenge is something that gives him the incentive to make things happen. A challenge is a risk. He may feel so ultimately responsible for the challenge to make the church grow that he has to fight failure if it does not. That is part of the risk, but the risk is exciting.

Church growth is dependent on personal growth because of a wholistic view of discipleship.—The eye is inoperative without the brain. The lungs cannot function without the heart. It is equally impossible to separate the function of discipleship into small entities. One does not suddenly discover that his arms are the only portion of his body that is growing, unless the body has become seriously deformed. The arms grow as the entire body grows. Personal growth does not happen as a separate part of growth for the Christian apart from church growth. The church is truly the incarnation of Christ in the present world. When the church grows, it is because persons who make up the church are growing. The leader is growing, and he is leading others to grow.

---

1. C. B. Hogue, *I Want My Church to Grow* (Nashville: Broadman, 1977), p. 31.
2. John F. Havlik, *The Evangelistic Church* (Nashville: Convention, 1976), p. 87.
3. "Growth in Grace," a sermon by John R. Claypool, December 31, 1978.

4

Growing in Self-Understanding

Alice said to the cat, "Would you tell me, please, which way I ought to go from here?" "That depends a good deal on where you want to go," said the cat. "I don't much care where—," said Alice. "Then it doesn't much matter which way you go," said the cat.

—Lewis Carroll, *Alice in Wonderland*

Where do you, as a minister, want to go? If you, like Alice, are not greatly concerned, direction is not really required. If, however, you want your church to grow and if you have certain goals in mind, you will need to grow personally.

Personal growth involves knowing who you are, what your needs are, how you behave, where you are going, and how to deal constructively with the various stages of your ministry. Apart from this meaningful kind of growth, you may be building a hollow, unsatisfying ministry. Meaningful personal growth has four basic characteristics; it is intentional, directional, dynamic, and relational.

Growth is intentional.—It is not automatic or inevitable; it is by choice. Times of dissatisfaction or crisis force a decision. Decision calls for a conscious risking, a faith leap, a letting go of one phase of life to begin a new dimension. Rather than just reacting to what life brings, you can set purposeful goals toward which your energy and resources are directed.

67

Growth is directional.—It is future oriented, a venture or pilgrimage. Christ being our model, we "press toward the mark for the prize of the high calling of God in Christ Jesus" (Phil. 3:14). Growth comes in passing successfully through certain stages as you move toward the fulfillment of life.[1] Successful passage or development in one stage brings preparation for the next.

Growth is dynamic.—It is not static; it is not reaching a fixed state. In fact, one growth characteristic is that the individual seems to become more content to be a process rather than a product.[2] A popular belief is that each person is born with a number of "givens," an inherited personality which sets that individual on a determined, no-change, no-control course of life. To the contrary, growth is a process of becoming, and, for the Christian, God is the Lord of the process.

Growth is relational.—You interact with yourself, your neighbors, and God. An important aspect of growth requires confronting your thoughts and feelings through self-examination. The risk involved is the fear of finding out things about yourself which are painful. However, the alternative is to disown your limitations, to pretend to be someone other than yourself. This dialogue with yourself is a prelude to sharing yourself with others. While being alone and introspective has great value, an equal value comes from sharing who you are with others. At risk here are the fear of admitting your imperfections, the threat of being rejected if others know what you are like, or the uncertainty of trusting others with knowledge of who you really are. Yet denying failures and imperfections also denies growth.

Personal growth concerns coming to a greater self-awareness, defining and clarifying ministry roles, dealing constructively with change, and examining mental and physical health. The purpose of the process is that you might come to a greater understanding of who you are and that you might build on that understanding.

Finding Self-Awareness

You have choice in the direction your life will go. But how do you decide where you want to go if you do not know where you are and from where you have come? The real purpose of self-awareness is self-actualization. The goals of self-actualization are for you to reach an optimal level of fulfillment, to be fully in charge of your life under God's direction, to trust your own judgments and emotions, to be candid with yourself, and to take responsibility for what you do in risking security and safety for growth.

Understanding who you are takes into account several factors. Part of your personal identity was shaped by formative influences, significant individuals, and experiences which were meaningful in your formative years. Other parts grow out of your personality, temperament, and behavior; those values which you hold and around which you build your life; your style of leadership based on your personality; and what you think of yourself (self-esteem). Examining these factors will help you determine which direction you wish to grow and what goals to set.

Formative Influences
Some people find their past to be painful; they hope to forget certain individuals or happenings which they have labeled "bad." Yet it is impossible to bury the past; it will reappear in your thinking, feelings, and behavior. A more constructive method is to make the past work for you. You can discover how your life's "script" was acquired.[3] Like an actor on the stage, you act off of the script you have acquired; you feel compelled to play out a role in life as a result of the transactions between significant individuals who were a part of your early life.

You will find it helpful to share some of these formative influences with a select number of trusted individuals. Out of a community of trust with people who know you, you can receive feedback for use in identifying specific patterns of personality, attitude, and behavior.

Bruce Larson suggested that another valuable use of the past for growth is for you to dedicate your past to God.[4] In leaving your past life in God's hands, you will find strength to grow from it rather than be victimized by it. Accept God's forgiveness where needed and his blessing where appropriate. With this attitude, finding your past should be a rewarding opening of self.

Personality, Temperament, and Behavior

Personality surveys, sometimes called tests or instruments, are helpful tools in taking an objective look at yourself. Surveys are generally constructed to deal with specific temperament traits, personality factors, and behavioral patterns. These surveys also help form a profile of your personality.

Several points are important in understanding personality surveys. First, get qualified persons to administer and interpret the instruments for you. Second, the results of any survey are not necessarily perfectly true. The results can be affected by how you felt when you took the test, your frame of mind, the situation, and your health. Finally, any survey you take on yourself is simply a reflection of what you are saying about yourself—how you think, feel, or behave. The results are not what someone else thinks; you are the one who answered the questions.

Attitude Identification

A part of who you are lies in the values you hold. These values form much of the basis for decisions. Problems in making decisions can arise from conflicts in values. Your values are those concerns which you hold most worthy.

A number of surveys or activities can help you identify and clarify your values. Maury Smith defines a full or real value as having seven criteria. First, you freely choose what you consider a full value; you do not simply accept it from your family, church, or society. Second, you select such a value from several alternatives. Third, you consider the effects of those alternatives. Fourth, you act on the basis of that value; you do not just hold a strong opinion about it. Fifth, you repeatedly make use of that value. Sixth, a full value helps you to grow, to develop toward your potential. Seventh, you share that value with others.[5] For a value to be real or full it must meet all seven of these criteria. Those interests or concerns which do not meet the criteria for a full value are partial values or value indicators. A partial value or indicator is in the process of being formed or growing such as a belief, opinion, attitude, or aspiration. Those things for which you use your most time and money are strong value indicators.

Self-Esteem

One of the most important aspects of self-awareness is understanding how well you accept and like yourself. Without an awareness of God's love and acceptance, you will find it difficult to love or accept yourself. You will constantly try proving to others that you are OK, strive to be perfect, or try outworking everyone. This is in actuality a sort of salvation by works. Though hardly any minister believes this, many practice it. If God loves you, you can love yourself. There is a big difference between loving yourself and being selfish. In fact, the Bible speaks of loving others as you love yourself.

Numerous self-assessment or self-concept exercises can help you become aware of how you perceive yourself. Some basic concerns are in the way you perceive who you are, how you accept yourself and your behavior in the areas of your physical self, your moral-ethical self, your intrinsic acceptance of yourself apart from your physical self, your family self, and your social self.

Three additional important areas of self-awareness involve knowing where you are in your spiritual growth, knowing yourself in interpersonal relationships, and knowing your leadership style. These areas are extensively covered in separate chapters of this book.

Self-awareness is a significant phase of personal growth. Understanding from where you come to be who you are sets the stage for where you wish to go. As a result of self-examination, you can identify certain needs or growth issues. From these you will need to pinpoint obstacles which prevent growth. Next, identify positive goals toward growth. Select individuals whom you feel can give you the greatest potential for growth; specify what you expect of them and in what ways they can be helpful.

At the Sunday School Board, the Career Guidance Section of the Church Administration Department offers an intensive eleven-day course in personal and professional growth. This course is provided several times each year to assist ministers in examining themselves in the manner described in this chapter. It also affords a community of trust and affirmation in which formative issues can be explored and related to numerous instruments in the areas of personality, values, leadership, and self-esteem.

Defining Ministry Roles

Every vocation or profession carries with it certain images of persons in that job and how they should behave. Physicians are expected to be tirelessly battling illness, and lawyers are supposed to act like Perry Mason. A part of your ministry involves the image others hold of you and which you hold of yourself. That ministerial image is often spoken of as a role.

The Roles of Personality and Function

Roles provide an understanding of who a minister is and what can be expected of him. As a minister you present images in two areas: your personality and your function. The personality role has to do with who you are. For example, many people see the minister most often in the pulpit; therefore they expect him to be an expressive talker at all times. Because of his dedication and calling, they expect him to be self-disciplined, concerned, and sympathetic by nature. The functional role is concerned with what you do. A congregation expects activity from you in three main areas: worship leader-preacher, teacher-counselor, and organizer-administrator.[6]

Roles Clarification

What happens when your personality is not the typical ministerial image or when the functional roles you think most important are different from those most appreciated by your congregation? Obviously a need exists to define your roles for the benefit of both you and the congregation. You as a minister came to your calling holding certain images of yourself as a man of God. When those expected images are inconsistent with the person you are or who you see yourself to be, you experience considerable stress of "incongruency."[7] Church members likewise hold certain expectations of your personality. Some of these may be as vague as being a "good" or a "spiritual" person.

You can respond to role stress in one of three ways. First, by overcompliance you may seek to totally adopt the image thrust upon you. In this way you will try to conform to all the expectations you or others place on you. Second, by rebellion you may seek to totally deny the image, rejecting the expectations which you feel deny your personhood or individuality. Third, by utilizing the roles, you may seek to understand them, reinterpret them, and handle them constructively and positively.[8] On the positive side of roles, note that people in need come to you initially because they hold certain ideas of your ministry. In many cases, role expectations can help you work more effectively with persons. Clarifying and redefining those roles will enable you to act with integrity, to be your own person and God's servant at the same time.

Lyle Schaller identifies twelve functional roles of the minister: teacher, counselor, administrator, evangelist, visitor, leader among leaders, *the leader* to give advice and guidance, community leader, example of personal and spiritual growth, denominational worker, worship leader and preacher, and enabler who facilitates the call and ministry of others.[9] Schaller also suggests a procedure whereby a minister and a pulpit search committee can discuss their role expectations. While this is an excellent method of understanding what a prospective church is looking for in a pastor, it is equally valid for use with the church you now serve. The process involves giving each participant a set of twelve cards, each listing a separate pastoral role. Every participant, including the minister, discards what are felt to be the four least important roles and then rearranges the remaining eight in order of priority. By tallying the results, it is possible to see individual as well as congregational expectations.[10] Such material is a simple tool for discussing those areas of difference or similarity. The purpose of such dialogue is to reduce the stress on the minister's part and conflict between expectations on the part of both pastor and people.

Much satisfaction or fulfillment in the ministry comes from

being comfortable with your role, finding growth personally as well as professionally.

Dealing Creatively with Vocational Maturation

Change is inevitable. Growth cannot come without change. The key to satisfaction in growth is to recognize changes as they occur and make the best use of them.

Different people have different growth needs. Those needs are complicated by the fact that needs vary at different stages in life. This is especially true for the minister in that he experiences a developmental process of stages through which he must pass. Erik Erikson lists four stages of the adult from adolescence through old age.[11] These stages can also be classified by developmental stages of the ministry.[12]

The first stage is young adult (late teens to age twenty-five). Major concerns are with identity as an individual and as a minister. The entrance or start-up phase of ministry is considered by some to be the most "determinative" crisis in a career.[13] No confidence of experience has come; the practice of ministry is entered with concepts and ideals from preparation for the work. Needs center around developing lasting relationships, particularly the selection of a mate. The young minister may have or look for an older minister who can serve as a guide and father figure.

The second stage is junior adult (ages twenty-five to forty). Major factors are stabilization and advancement. Basic needs are in areas of being intimate, establishing and maintaining deep relationships, and receiving self-satisfaction from others. At the same time, pressure is felt to advance vocationally, the "make it or break it" phase. Getting along with friends, church members, and fellow ministers aid this goal. A greater awareness is felt of the need to "own" one's faith, no longer satisfied with simplistic answers. A certain independence is gained, perhaps no longer depending on an older mentor.

The third stage is the mid-life adult (ages forty to fifty-fifty). The principle concern here is generativity or creativity, the "do it now or never" phase. Questions arise about what contributions are being made, what new ventures need starting, and what will be done with the rest of life. For some, concern for security is the greatest motivation. The mid-life stage can be a frightening time at home for the minister. Closeness with his children is sought just as they rebel in their independence. Rediscovery of his wife coincides with her move toward freedom away from home with the children gone. Yet this is a good time, for the wisdom of age has given perspective and understanding. At the same time, energy remains to create a legacy for the future. A number of books emphasize this stage, for example *The Mid-Life Crises of the Minister,*[14] *The Time of Your Life,*[15] or *The Middle-Age Crisis.*[16]

The fourth stage is the older adult (from about age fifty-five onward). The basic concern here is that of integrity or wholeness. The minister begins to transfer his hopes and ministry to younger pastors. His life-style becomes simplified and somewhat limited in income, health, or leadership. Nonetheless, he can continue to influence others, be productive, and serve. If health and finances are adequate, he may enjoy travel, hobbies, and a variety of interests.

Important considerations must be taken in adjusting to the changes of life and ministry. First, be aware of where you are and what you are to face in the future. Knowing the crises and opportunities can provide a measure of preparedness. An attitude of expectancy and hope can make a big difference in your approach to the passages through life. Second, be flexible so as to adjust, not break. Plan ahead financially, intellectually, and emotionally. Third, continue to learn. Stay alive by keeping up with what is going on. Fourth, maintain your spiritual-devotional life-style. Fifth, avoid taking yourself so seriously that you cannot relax and enjoy life. Sixth, seek to enrich and enjoy family life. Finally, search for new avenues of ministry to which you can devote yourself. If you are a mid-life adult, become a mentor for a younger son in the ministry.

Whatever your stage in the ministry, you may wish to consider a career assessment through the Career Guidance Section of the Sunday School Board. This experience may help you better to understand where you are and the direction in which God is leading you.

Maintaining Physical and Mental Health

Personal growth is set in the context of your physical and mental health. In fact, the rate or even the possibility of growth will largely be determined by the capacity of your mind and body to participate in the process. Any physical or mental limitation will by extension form a barrier to full actualization of your potential. Stewardship follows on this process as an appropriate use of the grace gifts God has provided.

Few of God's gifts are more precious than your mind and body. These are the instruments through which you serve God. Salvation does not come to your soul alone but brings redemption to every part of your being. Likewise, your call to minister is not limited to certain acts of service but is concerned with your entire personality.

The Body, a Vehicle of Ministry
A lingering stereotype of the Christian saint shows an ascetic whose body is at best a nuisance. According to this view, care for the body is unimportant; only the soul matters. Nothing could be further from biblical teaching. Exhortations concerning proper food and health care dot the pages of the Old Testament. Jesus called the disciples aside for proper rest. Many of Paul's instructions, particularly to the young minister Timothy, involved personal care. The nature of the ministry does expose you to a variety of stresses. Irregular schedules, anxiety-laden situations, prolonged low activity, and encouragement to overeating are common to most ministers. Such stresses require top physical condition to resist serious consequences to health.

Good health basically involves using good common sense in caring for yourself. Some serious illnesses can be avoided, but this requires a positive program of care. Three broad principles are useful: Know your physical condition; work toward physical fitness; and adopt a life-style which will maintain your fitness throughout your life.

Start by learning your present state of health. Have a thorough physical examination to assess your condition and to pinpoint any problems. Since weight level and exercise are vital to health, your doctor can assist you in determining your optimum weight and a sensible program of exercise. Further, physical conditions often influence behavior, attitude, and emotional response. A physical examination should identify any such conditions.

Physical fitness does not necessarily mean being skinny or skilled in sports. It simply means your body is functioning efficiently in its physiological systems.[17] Increasing your body's performance efficiency involves improvement in the cardiovascular-respiratory system, in muscular endurance, and in flexibility. A regular program of exercise will accomplish these results. Increased oxygen in the system will increase alertness, awareness, and adaptability to stress and change. Select some type of exercise which you enjoy and which you can practice on a year-round basis. The activity should be strenuous enough to increase your oxygen intake, strength, and endurance. How much exercise you can tolerate is determined by heart rate.[18] Use a reliable guide in setting up your program, and stick to it to avoid doing more harm than good.

Maintaining physical fitness means adopting a daily approach to life which is compatible to good health. Take a long look at your habits of rest, exercise, work, and diet. Bring them into good balance. Eating habits are especially helpful in weight control. Plan for long-term change rather than quick fads in exercise and weight control. Consult with your family; plan your fitness as you would any important area of your life. You can help protect yourself from disease, increase your life expectancy, and add vitality to your life now.

The Mind, a Transceiver of Reality

Mental health, and to a great extent physical health, is being in touch with reality.[19] Reality touches on wholeness, the God-given harmony of body, mind, and spirit that can be referred to as salvation. Reality sharpens our senses to the world around us and promotes a redemptive attitude toward ourselves and others. Such an attitude is vital to ministry. Mental health comes when you comprehend reality, apply it in self-awareness, and express it in relationships with others. This process brings stability, maturity, and purpose to life. Several broad principles of mental health summarize some ways you can go about getting in touch with reality.[20]

Accept who you are.—You are loved of God by right of creation, a partaker of his given worth. You are Christ's gift to the church, equipped to carry out your unique ministry. By taking an honest and accepting look at yourself, you can determine reasonable goals without either belittling or overestimating yourself.

Learn how you operate.—Try to determine how you respond to persons and situations. Identify how you express anger, joy, frustration, wants, and the like. Seek competent and reliable help in this process. How you operate forms a vital part of how others understand and react to you.

Get support from others.—Build a confidential relationship where you can be open. Sharing experiences, ideas, and anxieties frees you from feeling isolated. You might wish to start and maintain a support group for this end.

Accept other people.—Acceptance does not mean agreement with or submission to other persons. It does mean seeking to understand another's point of view. Sure of your own self-worth, you can take differences without feeling threatened by or challenged to dominate others. Get involved in group activities. Try to identify how others are feeling and what their needs are.

Look for alternatives.—Locate the options in any situation. Try new methods. Even if your method fails, you have learned. Use the same sensible, solid methods for attacking personal problems that you would use in your job.

Like your vocation.—Some aspects of ministry are more personally satisfying than others, but try to realize the value in all you do. Sense the accomplishment in your service. See the broad picture rather than get hung up on trivialities. Make sensible work plans. Set realistic goals for yourself and others. Find joy in knowing that what you are doing is right for you.

Be creative.—Find something to do which is satisfying or pleasing to you alone. Choose some form of art, craft, or skill that releases your inner self. Whatever you choose, do not make it labor or another job.

Be forgiven.—Trust in God's love. Seek after the abundant

life that is in Christ. Forgiveness and healing have been graciously given; accept them and grow in the strength they provide. Let your forgiveness be the spirit in which you reach out to others as God's servant.

1. Lewis J. Sherrill, *The Struggle of the Soul* (New York: Macmillan, 1977), p. 21.
2. Carl Rogers, *On Becoming a Person* (Boston: Houghton Mifflin, 1961), p. 22.
3. Muriel James and Dorothy Jongeward, *Born to Win* (Reading, Mass.: Addison-Wesley, 1971), p. 36.
4. Bruce Larson, *The One and Only You* (Waco: Word, 1974), p. 76.
5. Maury Smith, "Some Implications of Value Clarification for Organization Development," *The 1973 Annual Handbook for Group Facilitators* (LaJolla, Calif.: University Associates, 1973), p. 205.
6. James Glasse, *Putting It Together in the Parish* (Nashville: Abingdon, 1972), p. 56.
7. David Jacobsen, *The Positive Use of the Minister's Role* (Philadelphia: Westminster, 1967), p. 18.
8. Ibid., p. 40.
9. Lyle Schaller, *The Pastor and the People* (Nashville: Abingdon, 1973), p. 46.
10. Ibid., p. 47.
11. Erik Erikson, *Identity and the Life Cycle*, Psychological Issues Monograph Vol. 1, No. 1, pp. 89-98.
12. Robert D. Dale, *Stages in a Minister's Adult Life Cycle*, cassette tape, ℗ 1979 Broadman Press.
13. Charles Stewart, *Person and Profession* (Nashville: Abingdon, 1974), p. 76.
14. Ray W. Ragsdale, *The Mid-Life Crises of a Minister* (Waco: Word, 1978).
15. Myron C. and Mary Ben Madden, *The Time of Your Life* (Nashville: Broadman, 1977).
16. Barbara Fried, *The Middle-Age Crisis* (New York: Harper and Row, 1967).
17. Richard B. Couey, "How Do You Get Physically Fit?" *Church Recreation Magazine*, July 1977, p. 24.
18. Ibid.
19. John Hendrix, "We Have This Treasure in Earthen Vessel," *Church Administration*, July 1977, p. 22.
20. Laurance F. Shaffer and Edward J. Shoben, Jr., *The Psychology of Adjustment* (Boston: Riverside Press Cambridge, 1956), pp. 584-89.

5

Growing in Relational Skills

Jesus said the second greatest commandment is to "love your neighbor as you love yourself" (Matt. 29:39, GNB). The strong implication of this verse is that we need to feel loved in order to effectively love others. At its best, Christian love is a two-way street among God's professed people; it is to be mutually shared, especially if we are to keep growing.

As a minister and a friend of ministers, I have observed that we often assume that we have a large number of mutually supportive relationships. As ministers, we are involved in the lives of many people. However, closer examination reveals that many of those relationships are not necessarily mutually nurturing. These situations are certainly understandable because often the persons receiving our care and attention are for the most part unable to give much back to us in terms of personal support. Therefore, if we do not give conscious attention to our own needs and the ways of getting our interpersonal needs met, we find ourselves feeling burned out or driven by unrecognized motives. In such cases our own growth becomes arrested and our sense of joy and fulfilment diminished. It is not enough to assume that because we are helping others to grow that we are also allowing others to help us grow.

This chapter is about taking a serious look at our supportive relationships. Why do we need them? Who are these persons? How does one build or strengthen his personal support system? Am I really willing to accept support? What other means of support facilitate my growth as a minister?

Need for Personal Support

Recently I sat for eleven days with four ministers who in most circles would be considered successful Southern Baptist pastors. By successful, I mean that their annual reports looked good, their churches appeared to be healthy, and there were no movements within their churches to get rid of the preachers. We were dealing with personal and professional growth issues. There were some distinct differences in our theologies, life and ministry styles, criteria for effectiveness, and personality temperaments. However, we became a close-knit group of trusted brothers because we found some common ground of experience and feelings. For one thing we were all lonely people. We were not desperately lonely but definitely in need of some deeper, significant relationships—relationships with someone with whom we could tell it like we felt it without fear of being rejected or that the shared information would be used against us instead of for us. Realizing that this feeling of loneliness was important and pursuing its source got our group in touch with several of their growing edges. I have seen this kind of dynamic happen again and again when ministers become aware of some heartfelt needs and begin to share them in the presence of one another.

Baptist psychiatrist Louis McBurney pointed out in his book *Every Pastor Needs a Pastor* that ministers are human too and they have some common problems such as loneliness and isolation, unexpressed hostility, a sense of failure and inadequacy, job insecurity, and role confusion.[1] According to two Sunday School Board research projects 65.8 percent of pastors and 86.5 percent of ministers of education have experienced at least one major stress period in their job, career, family, and personal lives. In the survey of pastors, they were asked to list their most critical personal needs. The most frequently mentioned response centered around "the need for emotional support—to be accepted as a human being, to be loved, encouraged, and appreciated."[2] These kinds of needs are met in an atmosphere of true *koinonia*.

At this point my observation concurs with that of Mahan Siler. Significant growth does not usually happen unless one is a part of a dependable community of trusted others.[3] Growth means change, and to change means to move into the unfamiliar. The unfamiliar is scary and demands risk. In order to take such a risk, I need the offer of a caring, accepting relationship. Such a relationship may be offered by one person or by many. It may be established in a relatively brief time or over a long period of time. But without some such relationships growth is seriously crippled. Growth and healing have a lot in common; for example, neither happens in isolation.

Actually the need for significant relationships to facilitate our personal and professional growth is not new. God has always used significant others to help man experience him. First he used Abraham and the patriarchs, then the prophets and kings, and ultimately came himself in the form of his son Jesus Christ. Even though the term "relational theology"[4] may be recent, the concept and practice emerges from the well-springs of biblical theology. This is the method God intended all along.

Our faith implies that God knows how to meet our deepest needs. Hence by analyzing the transactions between God and man, we can learn a lot about how to relate effectively to one another. What are some of the basic dynamics that happen in God's relationship to man and that we can apply to man-to-man relationships?

The nature of a trusting community or significant relationship gives a lot of time and energy to seeking to know and understand one another. The power of feeling understood and of sensing you better understand another is potent indeed. For understanding to grow there needs to be a dependable level of acceptance and compassion. The compassion needs to be nonpossessive or as unconditional as possible (total unconditional love is possible only for God). Empathy, the ability to crawl into another's skin and experience life from his perspective, is a redemptive characteristic. This is especially true if you sense another person is accurately in touch with what you are feeling. Accurate empathy creates a bonding effect between two or more persons. Genuineness, being real, or taking off the masks with one another causes trust to grow. It produces more openness and honesty. Such an atmosphere helps dialogue to take place at a deeper level. These dynamics add up to a sense of mutuality and intimacy which needs to be held in healthy balance by enough individual freedom and distance to allow each individual to have and develop his own identity.

As a minister attempting to grow to become more like Christ and to be healed when I am hurting, I need a personal support system composed of a trusting community. Thus to choose to be committed to such a community is not to admit personal failure, overdependency on others, or even lack of trust in Christ; it is rather to respond to God's provision for helping me heal and grow. This does not mean I do not go directly to the heavenly Father with my needs, but it means that when I do ask for guidance many times he directs me to another human being. When Paul asked for direction, God sent him to men such as Ananias and Barnabas.

People Resources Who Make Up a Personal Support System

Once a minister has recognized the need and value for a personal support system, he will most likely ask, "Who is included in my personal support system?" A support system has several different levels. Generally these levels certainly would include one's spouse and family but also some friends both inside and outside the local church and peers or colleagues in vocational ministry.

I don't need everybody in all these levels to be in my support system—that's unrealistic and unreasonable. However, persons whose behavior toward me is consciously supportive I term as "significant others." By significant I meant that they seem to be willing to share openly with me and encourage me to share some personal matters with them. Also the significant other appears to value me as an individual, and I highly respect him as a person whose own values appear to be meaningful, personally valuable, and nonthreatening.[5] Such relationships always hold the promise of deeper sharing and mutual personal and interpersonal growth. For example, if I am struggling with a clearer sense of self-understanding, significant others enter the pilgrimage with me and give me caring feedback as to how they have and are experiencing me as a person. If I am in a lonely, depressed state, they become a sister or brother in Christ and temporarily loan me some of their strength and insight. Or if I'm failing to celebrate my ministry accomplishments or personal joys, they hold up to me the flowers of God's blessings and my share in them.

Those significant, other people are everywhere, if we look for them. Let's look at the specific levels on which they can stand with us.

Marriage Partner and Family
In one of the research reports mentioned above, when pastors were asked to indicate who was most helpful to them during stress, their wives were listed more than any other persons. When the pastors were asked to rank how much they valued the praise of each of seven persons or groups listed, wives again came out on top with an 82.9 percent ranking.[6] Such data verifies again and again how strategic spouses are to our need for personal support.

For a minister and his family to get the most mileage out of their potential for mutual support, they need to be aware of the issues which challenge the supportive process. I see these issues as challenges because how they are handled determines whether they become the means through which support is experienced or sabotaged. Some of these issues or felt needs appear to be common to all marriages, and others seem to be common to most ministers' families. The needs common to all Christian marriages are regarding:

- in-depth communication.
- expression of affection.
- handling of negative emotions.
- managing separateness and togetherness.
- providing opportunities for effective spiritual growth for the family.

In addition to these, other common needs which relate specifically to the minister's family are:

- lack of adequate quality time together.
- no assured privacy.
- conflicting and/or unclear role expectations within the congregation and the family itself concerning the minister's family, especially with regard to the wife and children.
- an inadequate supply and/or mismanagement of financial resources.
- the strain of always being a model of the ideal Christian.
- few close friends.

All these issues seem to be fairly normal though they are experienced with different intensity by different persons·at various times. Usually there are some other underlying interpersonal issues such as one's self-understanding and self-esteem that affect how he perceives those marriage-family issues.

Once we are willing to identify and accept responsibility for what our specific issues are, how we determine to deal with them is important. One technique out of creative problem-solving methodology which I have found helpful is to continue to redefine my felt need until I see it clearly. Then I am ready to own my need, to grow, and to begin to take other steps toward change.

The following section offers some practical suggestions concerning how to develop and reconstruct a support system. These suggestions can be adapted and applied to the marriage and family. However, some brief suggestions for meeting the challenges of support within the minister's family are in order here.

Lewis McBurney, the Baptist psychiatrist whose primary vocational function is counseling ministers and their families, has made some practical suggestions. There are four things a minister can do: (1) You need to give some *undivided* attention to your family. (2) You need to share intimately the real you (your life history, likes, dislikes, goals, and even your doubts, fears, and failings—deleting the x-rated parts). (3) Likewise your family need to feel that you understand them in some depth. (4) Finally they need to experience your expressions of affection; don't let all your attention be negative.

In addition there are some things the family itself can do: (1) The most effective step is to learn to communicate feelings and needs openly and honestly. (2) A preventive measure is that of evaluating the family's expectations of themselves and testing expectations against realistic and attainable goals. (3) The family needs also to encourage one another to build supportive friendships with persons with whom they can share openly their pain and joy. And finally, according to McBurney, the minister should educate the congregation concerning what his needs and pressures are.[7]

My experience has been that this education process can prove to be redemptive for both the congregation and the minister's family if it is done out of an attitude of valuing Christian priorities.

Ernest Mosley, in his book *Priorities in Ministry,* set forth the biblical priorities as being in the following order: A minister is: (1) a Christian person, (2) a married person, (3) a parent person, (4) a church member person, (5) an employed person, (6) a community person.[8] Acting out of such priorities is not only a good example, but it will ensure a more enriched personal and family life which is foundational to a more effective ministry life.

So there are some definite things ministers can do to build their base of support by reaching out to their marriage partner and children. In the process don't forget to receive from them as well as give to them. Ministers often discount or miss the strokes and nurturing their own families intend for them to have. Teenagers especially have subtle and nonverbal ways (that are both conscious and unconscious to them) of saying thanks and I love you.

Another source of support is the extended family which includes parents, grandparents, aunts, uncles, cousins, in-laws, and other kin. Usually there are several in this group who are vitally interested in us as persons and professionals. The extent of their support will depend not only on their interest but also on how often they are in touch. Persons can be greatly concerned about us, but their ability to be of significant support is limited if they are not there when we need them.

Sometimes after analyzing one's support system a decision is made intentionally to work on certain family relationships. Remember most ministers move from place to place, but the marriage-family relationships are more permanent. They are the first line of support. When they are not supportive, the entire support system is weakened. How is your support system on the home front?

Friends
Another level of personal support that facilitates growth is those significant, other persons usually known simply as friends. Jess Lair, the university professor and author of *I Ain't Well—but I Sure Am Better* says that in order to make one's spiritual quest in life he needs his wife, kids, family, and five good friends.[9] He tags these five friends as being persons whose faces light up when they see him. He goes on to describe these friends in terms of shared mutuality and acceptance. In other words they have some vital common interests and like you the way you are. They do not have a ready-made program for your self-improvement.

Can you name your five friends? We all know the value of hearing from a friend in a period when we need a boost. One of the predominant issues with many clergy families is the lack of close personal friends.

The issue is raised frequently concerning the tension between wanting intimacy with members of the congregation and the fear of the intrinsic dangers involved. Other members could become jealous and accuse the minister of being in a clique. Some ministers feel if they get too close and open members might lose respect for them. Others are concerned about being overinfluenced by their close friends in the church. These fears may become actual at times, but they can be guarded against. Church members can and must be educated to recognize the necessity for its leaders to have friends just as they need some close friends. In every church in which I ministered, I built friendships with some significant others who reached out to us out of their need or in helpfulness in our need. The church can come to recognize their minister's need to establish and maintain friendships without jealousy or possessiveness. Naturally some discretion must be used by the minister in the matter of friends within the congregation, but in most cases it can be managed if he is sensitive to the dangers.

Friends outside the church are also possibilities for support. Most ministers and their spouses do not have many because of the time involvement in the life of their own congregation and family. However, many are finding that having friendships outside the church gives them a different, even refreshing perspective. For one thing these friendships allow a break from church concerns that seem ever present. Also they can provide more objective support concerning issues that are peculiar to one's particular church or denomination. There are times when we need support from someone who is not as involved in a particular issue as we are to loan us some strength or insight.

Other friends may come in pairs. Couples' groups that meet mainly for fellowship and maybe food are popular among some ministers.

Most of us have some long-term or ongoing friendships that we have maintained from childhood, college, seminary, and former places of services. These friendships are especially meaningful if we can pick up where we left off on lasting meeting. The limitations of those relationships are usually due to the long distances that separate and infrequent visits. However, it is supportive to reflect on the reality that some folks have loved us over the long haul and still believe in us.

Old acquaintances are not enough. We need to continue to form present friendships. Sometimes for these to be supportive we have to work at developing them. When moving to a new location or a new stage in our growth, we have to search for new relationships. The past ones are not adequate for our present situation and needs. Often it takes a good deal of energy and time to test out new friendships. Many people do not reach out quickly or easily to ministers. Others reach out for less than mutually satisfying reasons.

There are different levels and durations of friendships. How wide and deep is your base of friendships? Are you giving and receiving the quality of support you need from your friends?

Peers and Colleagues
Some of the most affirming support comes from one's brothers and sisters who share a common calling. Often they best understand our problems, concerns, and victories. They know firsthand about ministry issues and the stress which at times has eternal implications.

Especially in our earlier ministry it is helpful to have a mentor in ministry to whom we can look for understanding, insight, and hope. These ministers are not only models but are also enablers, helping us over humps and seeing further down the road than we can see from our own perspective. As we move along the road of life, our mentors die or become more clay-footed brothers like us; but they are still just as important if not more so.

The ranks of colleagues may be fellow pastors and other staff members in our association. One's own staff is too often overlooked as a readily available support group. Part of the staff's contract with one another can be to function as an organized support group.[10]

Local denominational workers often are sensitive to the hurts and needs of local ministers, and many times they are aware of their need for support. Hopefully they are also aware of other resource persons and materials. One's peers in other helping professions outside of ministry are often willing to become brothers with ministers. Recently I was with a group of ministers who had invited a well-known, retired, psychology professor to be a part of them. Hospital chaplains have been some of the most open professionals with whom I have been able to relate. Usually there are many possibilities if we are willing to take the initiative to seek them.

Sometimes ministers are hesitant to reach out to their peers inside or outside ministry because of feelings of competitiveness or fear of betrayal or rejection. One study showed that Southern Baptist pastors and denominational executives were perceived as being the least supportive in periods of stress.[11] This is a sad commentary. There must be several reasons for it. One is that it is difficult to be both supportive and competitive at the same time. Therefore, we need to see ourselves not as competitors for reputation and influence but as colaborers in God's enterprise.

In some cases it may be necessary and preferred to reach across denomination lines for in-depth colleague support. One of the best support persons I had as a pastor was a Disciples minister who pastored in the same town as I did. My experience has been that when I have been willing to give the intentional time and energy I can discover peers both inside and outside the denomination with whom I have enough mutuality to begin to build trust and acceptance.

Formal Versus Informal Support

Most of us have a support system of some fashion. These persons have chosen to accept and encourage us. We have consciously or unconsciously chosen them as significant others. They have value and worth to us. However, because the need for personal support is so great in the pressurized world of the modern minister, he needs a system of both informal and formal support. The difference that distinguishes formal support from informal is that a formal support relationship is for the expressed purpose of being openly and mutually supportive. Now support can happen in informal ways in all relationships, but it usually happens more as a by-product of working, playing, or worshiping together. Whereas in the formal support relationship to be supportive is the primary objective. In other words support is worked out intentionally.

A formalized support relationship is not merely to provide opportunities for informal rap sessions. Rather the persons involved in formal support define their goals, measure their progress frequently, and celebrate that progress. They build the agendas for their meetings and define their structure and expectations.

Let me illustrate out of my personal experience what I mean by formal and informal support relationships. An example of an informal set of relationships is a married couple's group with which my wife and I are involved. The group is made up of several men who work in the Church Administration Department and their wives. Generally the group gets together once a month for eating and fellowship. It is enjoyable and as supportive as social relationships can be. We talk about things that are happening at work and in the lives of our families. Seldom does anyone share anything deeply personal. Attendance is sporadic; commitment to the group is short-term. I want to continue to be a part of this group, but I also must continue to realize that in terms of in-depth personal support and closeness the group has its limits.

On the other hand, I am a member of two different formal support groups. These groups have a clearly defined, systematic structure for giving and receiving support. Each member has made a clearly stated and strong commitment to the group. Our overall objective is to develop and deepen the levels of understanding, acceptance, sharing, and caring with one another. Attendance is almost 100 percent; the motivation to be involved is high. I have given much of myself to these persons, and I have received much support from them.

A formalized support group may organize around a specific interest or specialized focus of mutuality. Couples interested in marriage enrichment, a church staff interested in team building, a therapy group whose interest is in personal growth and healing, or a task or study group can covenant to become a formal support group. One of my support groups is focused around the professional interest of pastoral counseling. The other group focuses more on the concern of our own personal growth.

There is some concern among professional group leaders as to whether issues relating to both personal growth and professional growth can be adequately dealt with simultaneously in the same group. I think that one or the other should be the primary focus; but since a growing person is a whole person, it is difficult, if not impossible, not to deal with both the personal and professional aspects. My professional effectiveness is greatly influenced by my self-actualization as a Christian person, but also my sense of personal worth is strongly affected by my professional effectiveness.

Both informal and formal expressions of support are necessary. It is helpful to know the difference. As a result you will be able to keep your expectations more clear. Sometimes we expect too much from people who can support us only informally.

Since supportive relationships are so vital to one's growth, let's examine how these relationships are formed and developed into being as redemptive as humanly possible.

Guidelines for Developing Personal Support Relationships

There are some functional guidelines to apply in developing either informal or formal support relationships. In a formal relationship these guidelines become acted on more explicitly. The guidelines are usually more or less assumed and acted on with less reflection in an informal relationship.

Analyze Your Present Support System

A beginning step is assessing how your support system is doing the job. Are your needs for encouragement, support, and growth being met adequately? Even if you already are consciously aware of your support system, it is good periodically to evaluate your supportive relationships.

One way to do that analysis is to ask yourself some reflective questions about the quantity and quality of support that you are or are not receiving. The questions might be along the following line: How comprehensive is my support system? Who are the ten most supportive people in my personal life? Who are the ten most supportive people in my professional life? How accessible are these persons when I need them? How much depth and closeness is there in our relationship? Are each of these persons aware of what I need from them? Do I have a formal support group? What support needs am I seeking to get met from each of my support persons?

These assessment questions revolve around the issues of the breadth, depth, and regularity of our supportive relationships. We need to answer the questions and others like them by listening to our gut-level feelings and not fooling ourselves by telling it like we wish it were or like it once was. After we have made an honest assessment, we are more able to move on to the next guideline.

Choose Your Support Persons or Groups

Whether you decide to develop informal or formal support relationships or both, there are some common things to consider. You will want to find some persons with whom you have some common interests. A good dose of mutuality and acceptance should be there from the start even though it will grow as time goes on. At the same time a support relationship is not for the purpose of fostering like-mindedness. Therefore the similarities need not be the same viewpoints, opinions, or giftedness. Persons or groups who are too homogeneous can be unchallenging and uncreative, while groups that are too heterogeneous can contain so much threat that individual growth can be held back or swallowed up in the energy given to maintain the group's interpersonal issues.

The options of choices will come from the many different levels of your relationships. You may decide to experiment and test becoming more human at a deeper level with some select members of your congregation. Or you may have discovered that you do not have a clear agreement with your marriage partner concerning your mutual support, and you choose to dialogue with her about that primary need. On the other hand, you might determine to begin to build or strengthen a formal support group consisting of your staff members or other colleagues in the ministry.

Choose whom you contact carefully and remember that no one should be pressured or required to join a formalized support group.

Contract the Support Covenant
Contracting a covenant is the act of drawing together an agreement between two persons, a person and a group, or two or more groups. In the case of informal support, this would be done more unceremoniously; but I do think it is productive to let the significant other persons know that you count on them for some supportive kinds of behavior. Such a conversation would provide the opportunity to tell them why you have selected them and express your gratitude toward them. They will also probably want to know more specifically what you want from them. You can also share what you will give to them in mutuality. I have found these conversations to be redemptive.

Contracting the covenant in a formal support group is usually more systematic and exact. If you are invited to join a support group already in existence, make sure you understand the terms of the covenant. If you decide to help start a group, the covenant issues to be determined are: (1) the focus of the group, (2) the meeting time and place, and (3) the format for the meetings.[12] The focus of the group should be decided after a discussion of felt needs, interests, hopes, and expectations. The frequency of support group meetings is important. Most ministerial groups meet weekly or semimonthly for approximately two hours each time. The place of meeting can be changed if the original location is not satisfactory. How the group will structure its time is a key decision. Some groups die or falter for lack of structure that leads to low-risk rap sessions; others superimpose a too structured format that does not allow for spontaneity and the pursuing of imminent needs.

Other issues to be determined in support group covenanting are size of membership (usually not over twelve, average is five to eight), when new members can come into the group, and the longevity of the group itself. Periodic evaluation sessions will help keep the group's covenant current with their needs.

Sometimes the question arises concerning whether a group covenant should be written or oral. That is up to the individuals involved. The important guiding factor is that the commitments are made clearly and that they are mutually satisfying and growth producing.

Pay Attention to the Redemptive Process

There is a process that happens when persons seek to relate to one another in a supportive way. Some extraordinary dynamics begin to move among these persons. In such an atmosphere the attempts to know and understand one another begin to build a deepening mutual trust. A growing understanding brings a fuller acceptance. This acceptance creates a security in which members can feel more free to share themselves more openly with the group. Out of this understanding, trust, acceptance, and sharing the group members come to care for one another. This whole process is redemptive.

Psychiatrists call this the therapeutic process. Among Christian brothers and sisters it can be called the redemptive process in recognition of the divine influence in relationships.

It is important to recognize this relational process and pay attention to it. It will help you rejoice in your individual and interpersonal growth and to be able to evaluate and change individual and group behavior which sabotages growth. Occasionally and momentarily along the way, diagnose the amount of acceptance and closeness in your group. How does each member react to the others? What sense do you make out of their behavior and attitudes? How much does each member influence the group? Are the individuals willing to follow as well as take some responsibility for the group? Is there a good deal of nonpossessive compassion shown? Do the members empathize on a deeper feeling level with one another without being overprotective or losing their objectivity? Is there enough freedom to risk oneself to be genuine with the group? If these interpersonal dynamics are developing, the group process is in good functioning order for God to facilitate some redemptive growth and change.

Practice Growth-Producing Koinonia

Koinonia is the New Testament term which describes in-depth fellowship. There are two group practices which facilitate the growth of *koinonia* and thus the growth of the individuals involved. The first is mutual self-disclosure. This is the practice of what the late Carlyle Marney called "the spinal cord of redemption. The nerve to submit all my images of the self to Christ and his people for correction."[13] Each member in a supportive relationship must be guaranteed times when he will have and take the opportunity to share more of his hidden self with these significant others. This mode of operating energizes the group's redemptive process.

The other practice is that of asking the significant others for honest feedback as to how they perceive one another's knowledge, attitudes, and behavior. This feedback will consist both of graceful confrontation and affirmation. It is through this process that one's blind spots will be brought to his attention enabling him to do something about them.

These two practices, giving self-disclosure and asking for feedback, are the acting out of *koinonia* in-depth.

Several state conventions have support groups for ministers. Some of these groups are constructing some helpful materials.

State minister-church relations directors or state church adminis-tration consultants can offer some resources. The Career Guid-ance Section of the Church Administration Department has resources available.

Willingness to Accept Professional Support

In the Sunday School Board study of pastors and stress, 57.7 percent agreed with the statement, "I sometimes find I would like counseling help to deal with my personal problems and con-flicts."[14] Many ministers feel this need, but it is often difficult for them to seek out the actual resources. The stigma is still with us that the man of God should not have feet of clay. In a 1978 minister's family survey conducted by the Board, approximately one third of 310 pastors' wives indicated that they would not feel free to visit a mental health or marriage counselor if they felt the need to do so.[15]

Although the barriers to seeking professional help for career, individual, and marital-family counseling are still there, Southern Baptists are slowly breaking them down. One of the ways is by offering assessment and counseling services across the Conven-tion. Several state conventions now have church-ministry rela-tions directors who either provide actual counseling or make responsible referrals to well-qualified counselors. In some cases they even subsidize the costs. The Career Guidance Section of the Sunday School Board's Church Administration Department offers professional help through its programs of Personal and Pro-fessional Growth and Career Assessment. This section also main-tains a referral network listing to help ministers and their families get caring, responsible ministry. National organizations such as the American Association of Pastoral Counselors and the Ameri-can Association of Marriage and Family Therapists will furnish names of certified counselors within driving distance of any place in the Convention.

When selecting a counselor, get recommendations from per-sons who have used his services, inquire about his training and theology or philosophy of counseling. My personal preference is for counselors whose training has included several hours of close supervision. The counseling field is becoming invaded by self-trained counselors who often get the counselee's problems all mixed up with their own.

The key is not to wait too long before you reach out for help. Remember that to confess your imperfectness and need for divine and human help is biblical. Usually it is our fear or pride that keeps us from accepting the support of other professional helpers. Most professional helpers will admire and understand your reaching out to them because they too have been in counseling at one time or another, either during their training or during a time of personal problems.

Awareness of Other Means of Support

In a recent pastors' review committee meeting, one member said, "I don't think the pastor should have to be concerned with money; he has more important problems that need his attention." I agreed with my generous brother ideally; but the fact is that most ministers are concerned about their compensation and other physical resources, and rightly so since these resources are vital to their personal support.

Ministers and their spouses usually list financial needs in the top five priority, critical, personal needs. Although ministers are aware of the need for adequate physical resources, few feel secure in their negotiating skills in the area. On this issue the local church, the denominational agencies and institutions, and the minister must work together.

The denomination can provide services and can help educate the congregation. Agencies like the Baptist Annuity Board can provide helpful services through retirement and insurance plans. Seminaries, the Seminary Extention Department, and the Sunday School Board can provide continuing educational opportunities which can help the minister discover his specific needs and sharpen his skills in developing support. Several denominational organizations from the associational to the Convention level can help the minister educate his local church. For example, compensation studies have been made on state and Convention levels that will allow a church personnel or finance committee to compare their staff compensation and benefits with other churches of comparable size. Denominational agencies are becoming more tuned in to their responsibility to aid and support the Southern Baptist minister. However, there is still a long way to go.

In the end, the minister must be willing to do his part in seizing the opportunities that help develop his support system and thereby help him to grow. For one thing he can claim his own need for physical support openly. There is always the tension that holds this process in healthy balance—the needs of the minister and his family and the resources and mission of the congregation. The minister has the job of being a good steward of himself, his family, and the church. One thing he can do is to make his needs known appropriately through the proper church committee channels. And do not forget needs in addition to the regular salary and allowances (car, housing, conventions, books). Some ministers are opting for and getting mini-sabbaticals (three or four weeks per year) for conference and enrichment time. And vacation time and days off to be with family and occasionally by yourself are necessary for growth and need to be in the agreement with the church. My pastor does a good job of linking up stategic leaders in our church with denominational personnel whose job it is to provide helpful information concerning ministry support.

Without the excesses of selfishness or poor stewardship, claim your right and responsibility for personal support from all available resources. It is more blessed to give than to receive; but if you fail to receive what God has provided, you cut off his means for your life's support systems. When you no longer have personal support, you dry up from the inside out and lose the joy of living and serving. To claim and develop your system of personal support is to accept the lifeblood that flows from God through others. Then you have something more to pass on to others.

1. Louis McBurney, *Every Pastor Needs a Pastor* (Waco: Word, 1977), pp. 61-75.
2. *The Critical Personal Needs of Pastors*, Research Services Department, Sunday School Board, June 1976, p. 8.
3. H. Mahan Siler, "The Growth Spiral: a Model for Pastoral Intervention," *Search*, Winter 1979, p. 27.

4. *Relational theology* is a term popularized in the writings of Bruce Larson, Keith Miller, and Carl Olson. An example is Bruce Larson, *The Relational Revolution* (Waco: Word, 1976). Also helpful is Doug Manning, "Relational Theology: Its Meaning for Southern Baptists," *Search,* Summer 1976, pp. 6-13.

5. Kenneth R. Mitchell, *Psychological and Theological Relationships in Multiple Staff Ministry* (Philadelphia: Westminster, 1966), p. 114.

6. *The Critical Personal Needs of Pastors,* pp. 4-5.

7. Louis McBurney, "Minister Support Is More Than Money," *The Quarterly Review,* Jan. 1979, p. 1.

8. Ernest E. Mosley, *Priorities in Ministry* (Nashville: Convention, 1978).

9. Jess Lair, *I Ain't Well—but I Sure Am Better* (Greenwich, Conn.: Fawcett, 1975), pp. 25-26.

10. Jerry W. Brown, *Church Staff Teams That Win* (Nashville: Convention, 1979), p. 96.

11. *The Critical Problems of Pastors,* pp. 4-5.

12. Howard Kirschenbaum and Barbara Glaser, *Developing Support Groups: a Manual for Facilitators and Participants* (La Jolla, Calif.: University Associates, 1978), pp. 23-27.

13. Carlyle Marney, *Priests to Each Other* (Valley Forge: Judson, 1974), p. 74.

14. *The Critical Problems of Pastors,* p. 5.

15. *The Minister's Family,* Research Services Department, Sunday School Board, September 1978, p. 15.

6

Growing in Leadership Skills

Many persons view effectiveness and efficiency as synonymous terms. They are not. Effectiveness is focusing on results as the final evaluation of success or failure in any operation. Efficiency may appear to be interested in results, but the emphasis is on how rather than what is being accomplished. A minister may arrive early each day to work, be neat in his office operation, and punctual in all correspondence; these are all works of efficiency. But unless he can use his time to the maximum, find what he wants when he wants it, and communicate so that others understand him, he is not results oriented, not effective. The proper use of facilities, time, people, and resources to accomplish an objective will ensure his effectiveness as a growth leader.

The skills most needed to be an affective growth leader are relational or people skills. The question to be answered is, How do I become effective or results oriented in my skills as preacher, counselor, educator, and administrator?

Leading Skills

The leading role of the minister is the motivating and directing responsibility. This is the ability of the manager: either to present an idea or to draw an idea from the group, to move to some sort of group action with the group idea, and to conclude a productive result as an end to dealing with the idea. The leader will evaluate his role on the basis of how he feels about the use of power and authority. If the leader assumes total authority, he violates the self-image and worth of those he leads. If the leader assumes no authority, he abdicates his responsibility and violates concepts of leadership which get work done. The leader that follows a democratic approach seeks to balance his use of authority and the freedom of the group.

Effective leading is dependent on the climate set for the activity to be performed. A positive leading climate is recognized in collaboration and teamwork when one feels people are working together toward commonly shared and accepted goals.

How to Become an Effective Leader
- Create a positive tone. Model a positive, enthusiastic stance.
- Be fair. Demonstrate a golden rule attitude.
- Be keenly aware of human feelings. Start with your own as a basis for knowledge.
- Be approachable, friendly. You can be best friends with those you lead.
- Treat each person as an individual. Each person is as unique as you are.
- Give praise. Positive affirmation works as well as negative.
- Take the attitude that all want to contribute. A slow response may come from the most committed participant.
- Be a good listener. Active listening reflects both feeling and content.
- Ask before demanding. A please is always appropriate at all levels.
- Be deliberate, organized, and steady. The discipline will improve you and the mission.

How to Remain Effective
- Be interested in individuals. People are more important

than things. Don't give the impression of using people.

• Work to be a friend. Take time to relax and generously show love.

• Demonstrate support for your team. Convince followers of your support and care.

• Control the quality of the group's actions. Be willing to confront and deal with inappropriate or poor response.

• Demonstrate success. Show your winning self.

• Act as leader. Be decisive. Take action.

• Speak as a leader. Don't be hesitant to assume the leader's role.

• Build your team. Take time to get the kind of people that work best with you.

• Admit your own errors; everyone knows anyway.

How to Know When You're Effective

• Things go smoothly, decently, and in order.

• Cooperation is better with fewer adverse reactions.

• Followers help one another. Cooperation takes the place of competition.

• There is good natured teasing and talk. People enjoy their work and find joy in participating.

• Complaints are reduced, and problems are solved. Change is welcomed and trusted.

How to Give Instructions

Leading in most instances is giving instructions or directions. These suggestions ensure effectiveness:

• Pick the right person to receive instructions. Make certain the enlisted person fits his position appropriately with the right abilities, skills, and knowledge.

• Be specific in setting expectations. In a staff meeting explain in detail your desire for improvement in a certain area. Don't leave room for guesses.

• Give a time frame. Tell when an activity is due and intended to be completed.

• Verify your instructions and directions by looking for understanding and feedback of the task.

● Follow up with continued interest, added explanation, and praise after accomplishment.

Communicating Skills

Talking, listening, giving, and requesting feedback are all part of the communication process. Communicators are influenced by their view of themselves, the other person, and each other together. What they know or don't know about each other is a factor along with goals realized or unrealized.

The ineffective communicator may be very talkative. He is probably living under the delusion that what he has to say is more important than what anyone else has to say. He may think he is expected to talk a great deal and therefore feels uncomfortable listening. Not to talk is to indicate a lack of knowledge. A minister may take his prophetic position of preaching into his other contacts and expect to be effective in one-way communication. He might assume that since others are quiet when he is around they want him to do all the talking, but the opposite is probably true.

The contrast of the talker is the futile communicator. To listen is to accommodate or comply with anothers' communication. This person will deny self and communication interaction by giving up his right and responsibility to participate. Listening becomes inactivity. This communicator relinquishes his influence to others. He thinks, *Who am I to say something in this setting? If I speak in this committee meeting, they will know I don't have the answer.* "Children are to be seen and not heard" is carried over into his adulthood. His low self-esteem encourages him to be quiet. This polite presentation may look like a high regard for others, but rather it is a low regard for self.

Another ineffective communicator seeks to be destructive in his approach. He neither listens nor talks but rather reacts by pouting, sulking, or in some way acting out his feelings in a negative, blocking manner. The objective is, Since I didn't get my way, be assured that no one else will get his way either. He operates out of hurt, resentment, selfishness, or some other self-serving ego state. Fight or flight becomes the order of the day which eventually immobilizes all fruitful communication attempts.

Productive communication depends on two communicators' willingness to approach the task in a positive manner. A productive communicator is not always assured that another person or group will use the same approach or skill. An individual can therefore only be responsible for his own behavior in attempting to be effective, recognizing that good communication will not occur unless both individuals assume the same stance. Modeling and demonstrating productive communication skills will sometimes lead both persons to success and effectiveness in communication.

This communicator will seek to explore and solve the problem in his attempts to relate. He views himself as important along with other persons. All have feelings, needs, and concerns. No attempts to control or get one's way is expected. Win-lose notions are excluded and instead win-win is the intended goal. Understanding is foundational; therefore, it is imperative that one be able to think how another person thinks or feels.

Talking and listening become processes. They are means to an end, and the end is effective relating. This sharing of influence gives both persons self-esteem. A greater goal is accomplished because each participant has input, and each person owns the results of the communication. The conclusions reached use sensitivity and empathy to appreciate the others' perspective. Developmental communication is the name for this approach since both talking and listening lead to a developed perspective.

These suggestions lead to effective communication:

1. Keep in touch regularly with those you lead and influence.

2. Check out feelings along with understanding in communication attempts.

3. Look for silent or unspoken messages through body language.

4. Allow for patience in difficult communication processes.

5. Watch for barriers to communication such as hidden agendas, double messages, or language differences. Sometimes these cannot be overcome.

6. Be willing to risk being open and honest.

Organizing Skills

Organizational management is generally limited to identifying work areas, properly classifying them, and establishing sound relationships between groups. All these activities involve the proper grouping of people.

Several giveaway indicators are present in deficient organization:

1. Frequent changes in plans, such as one approach for visitation after another.

2. Lack of succession in leadership, such as departments in Sunday School without leaders.

3. Late decisions, such as announcements in worship service not thought out.

4. Lack of accountability, such as when the staff assumes control of all divisions.

5. Excessive tenure, as one man serving twenty years as a Sunday School director.

6. Tolerance of incompetence, as when a visitation program has no one participating.

7. Recognition inequities, as noted when certain leaders receive all the attention and praise.

These and other problems stress the importance of using principles that support good practice in organizational development. The following list is offered as foundational in dealing with this ministerial skill area:

Be objective.—Every organization and every part of every organization must be an expression of the purpose of the undertaking concerned, or it loses its meaning. A weekday ministry that is not supported by the church is not a part of the church but simply is meeting there.

Specialize.—The activities of every member of any organized group should be confined, as far as possible, to the performance of a single function. When members have numerous jobs, they show diminished quality of performance due to the spread of responsibility.

Coordinate.—The purpose of organizing as distinguished from the purpose of the undertaking is to facilitate unity of effort.

A greater accomplishment can occur when work is organized to coordinate and correlate.

Authorize.—In every organized group the leadership role must rest somewhere. There should be a clear line of authority from the leader to every individual in the group. Clear lines of authority can be drawn in each organizational unit in the church.

Define.—The leader is responsible for the acts of his group. The pastor is the chief official and ultimately responsible for the church staff.

The content of each position, the duties involved, the authority and responsibility contemplated, and the relationships with other positions should be clearly defined in writing and published to all concerned. Job descriptions make expectations clearer for both the one positioned and for those who work with him.

Correspond.—In every position the responsibility and the authority should correspond. One cannot act responsibly without adequate authority.

Control.—No person should supervise more than five or six direct subordinates whose work interlocks. It is better to be closely related to a few key persons rather than to be all things to all people.

Balance.—It is essential that the various units of an organization be kept in balance. If one organizational unit becomes prominent, it may overpower and diminish emphasis on other units or functions.

Continue.—Reorganization is a continuous process, and specific provision should be made for it. Organization helps persons accomplish goals in the most effective way, and change is often necessary.

Organizational effectiveness is the result of blending integrated activity, competent people, common goals, purpose, and commitment to work together. The successful minister will master this skill.

Training Skills

The equipping role of the minister is as crucial as the proper enlistment of persons to fill positions. More damage can occur if an individual is enlisted to do a job and not trained to function properly than if the job were not filled in the first place. The minister who has the ability to train effectively will see each opportunity of enlistment as a time to grow people rather than to do things.

If a minister trains, he will model and set the stage for training throughout the church. Followers may see training as a negative designed to shape up, fill in, or fix the broken. If training has been given a positive stage in the church, it will be designed to go beyond, turn on, and seek out new heights. Training can be seen as something that was done once, as in a degree from a certain school, or as something that continues throughout life. The latter is the more productive because it stays up-to-date and is related to the present set of circumstances or position.

Effective training, led by the minister, can be accomplished on several levels:

Self-study training.—Book reading plans, cassette tape programs, videotape programs, and programmed learning items are all applicable to the individualized study approach. They can be designed so that the minister can provide modules for various training needs such as secretarial, counseling, or supervising.

Small-group training.—Church staff meetings, church council meetings, and committee meetings serve as opportunities for training. Inclusion of short, concise training experiences can be a part of regular business meetings by church leaders.

Ongoing studies and programs.—Church Training, Sunday School, WMU, Brotherhood, and Music offer training on a regular basis. These can be used to fit the need of any church leader discussing training.

In-depth training.—Seminary, workshops, lectures, and courses for professional growth are available in both the religious and the secular setting. Often these meetings can be conducted in the church building in cooperation with other churches or businesses.

On-location training.—Colleges, seminaries, and businesses provide training. Depending on the need, this getaway to the location of choice may be most appropriate for church leaders.

Recently the Church Training Department of the Sunday School Board introduced the concept of Equipping Centers. These are designed to provide training on the basis of meeting needs of groups and individuals with the most specific helps available. A leader would be wise to direct this program as a major channel for group and individual improvement.

Conflict Resolving Skills

One of the major skill areas of a dynamic church leader is that of conflict resolution. Use the following checklist to give organization to this process:

1. Preparation
- Get the facts straight.
- Decide what you want to achieve through interaction.
- Try to anticipate the reaction you are likely to get, and plan your approach accordingly.
- Prepare yourself mentally to absorb negative feelings if they surface.
- Double-check relevant policies, procedures, and previous agreements.
- Plan how you will bring up the subject.

2. Timing
- Choose a time of day to initiate conversation when the other individual is receptive.
- If you are angry about the other's conduct, cool off first.
- Do not piggyback your conversation on top of another conflict.

3. Setting
- Be honest and sincere, and above all be fair.
- Approach the disagreement like a problem two people have to solve, not a contest.
- Be diplomatic in your choice of words.
- Maintain firm control of your anger.

4. Communication
- Ask open-ended questions about the situation; try to understand the other's point of view.
- Be a good listener.

- Continually clarify what you think you are hearing to avoid misunderstanding.
- State your position clearly, and see if it has been heard.
- Accept responsibility for good communication, instead of blaming when there is a misunderstanding.
- Hang in there; take as much time as necessary within reason.
- Stick to the issue at hand.

5. Agreement
- Push for a complete, mutual understanding on what is to be done.
- Clarify points of agreement as they are reached.
- Be open to suggestions about what you can do differently in the future.
- Summarize the complete agreement before ending the interview.

6. Follow Through
- Do promptly what was promised.
- Seek out reactions of the other person to actions that have been taken.
- Be sensitive to the recurrence of a similar problem.

While these are but a few of the skills necessary for a minister, they do represent some of the most important ones. The master of these skills, plus a strong foundation or philosophy of working with people, is necessary for success. The skills used in growing ministers are varied. The priority of relationships does not change; only the setting changes. Ministers will grow if they succeed in the effectiveness of influencing, guiding, and directing people.

7

Growing as a Person in Christ

Spiritual growth is essential to the effective minister, not optional. Spiritual growth is possible in the context of ministry to people and is natural for the minister who manages well the relationships of life.

The price to be paid for the failure to grow spiritually is too great. It is an unnecessary price, since Jesus has made his presence, strength, and wisdom available to all those who follow him. It is an unlikely price for ministers who are deliberate about maintaining personal priorities in a way that honors the need for one's own spiritual growth and organizes time and relationships to meet spiritual growth needs.

Jesus' invitation to all his disciples is to join in a relationship that produces spiritual growth. This invitation was first spoken to Simon and Andrew (see Mark 1:16-18). They were called to go with Jesus in a life that would result in significant personal growth. Rather than continuing to be preoccupied with success in fishing boats or fish markets, they became preoccupied with success in helping persons to live.

The success of Simon and Andrew can be measured in the way they managed three relationships. First, they grew in relationship to Jesus. To follow him initially required trust. To stay with him through all that happened required growing trust and produced growing understanding. Second, each grew in relationship to himself. Following Jesus helped them learn more about their personal values, their fears, and their ability to endure as Jesus' disciples. Simon and Andrew were given the hope that they could become something more valuable than they were. Third, the disciples grew in relationship to other persons. To be able to relate effectively to their neighbors, to persons in all walks of life and all social and economic circumstances, is growth. To call attention to the news about Jesus Christ so that people could be drawn to him is evidence of their growth in relationship to Jesus and to themselves. As disciples who could effectively introduce others to Jesus and guide them in the way of life Jesus introduced, they grew personally.

To feel within themselves the abundance of the good life Jesus promised was the invitation to spiritual growth in all of its dimensions. This first-century encounter exposes to twentieth-century ministers the calling to personal, spiritual growth that is prerequisite to a life of effective ministry.

The personal need for the minister's spiritual growth is not the only issue at stake; there is congregational need as well. The minister's personal growth builds a foundation off which effective leadership can be provided. If the leader is growing in awareness of God and of self, there will naturally be growing awareness of other persons and their needs. There will be a commitment to helping persons grow rather than to using persons and wearing them out in efforts to reach organizational goals.

Ministers who are growing spiritually are aware that man was not made for the church but the church for man. These ministers lead in the development of organizational relationships, projects, and goals that foster spiritual growth in persons. They use the things of the church to serve persons rather than asking the persons of the church to serve things.

Another reason the church has a lot at stake in the minister's spiritual growth is because of the power of a model. No teaching method is more powerful than modeling. Alert Christians are turned off by life-style signals that communicate, "Don't do as I do; do as I say do."

The minister who is experiencing the power of Christ in personal life will be noticeable. That is not to imply that attention will be consciously called to one's spiritual growth. It does mean that just as " a city that is set on a hill cannot be hid" neither can a life that is experiencing spiritual growth. When the fruit of the Spirit (see Gal. 5:22-23) is present, people will know that something is unusual about a person's life. They will seek to know how life can be that way. They will desire that quality of life for themselves. The doors of opportunity will open, and the minister will be able to help church members grow spiritually. Then the rewards of one person's spiritual growth can be seen in the lives of persons throughout the church.

Spiritual Growth Is a Personal Responsibility

The subtitle of Richard J. Foster's book, *Celebration of Discipline*, suggests that spiritual discipline is "the path to spiritual growth." The first chapter begins by spotlighting a spiritual growth problem. "Superficiality is the curse of our age. The doctrine of instant satisfaction is a primary spiritual problem. The desperate need today is not for a greater number of intelligent people, or gifted people, but for deep people."[1] Superficiality may result from an unwillingness to pay the personal price required for spiritual growth. The fact that we will always be beginners in the spiritual growth world, with an unexplored world of potential around us, means that we always must be paying the price of learning and growth.

Develop Spiritual Growth Goals

We are most likely to succeed if we develop some spiritual growth goals for our lives. They should include both the North Star goals that express the person we want to become and the next-step goals that represent the step up the ladder of becoming. Setting challenging goals also calls for planning for regular and practical evaluation of progress toward the attainment of our goals. Many participants in worship services have become inspired to renew their commitment to Jesus and to become mature Christians. However, the desired spiritual growth got lost in the confusion of everyday living because they lacked a specific plan for growing toward spiritual maturity and for reviewing their progress at appropriate intervals. Satan is never alarmed at our occasional, serious rededications; but he fears defeat when we set out on the well-chartered course to spiritual growth that is introduced in the Scriptures and documented in human experience.

In *Priorities in Ministry* Ernest Mosley suggested a framework for setting spiritual growth goals and for evaluating progress toward the attainment of these goals.[2] Paul's identification of the fruit of the Spirit provides nine qualities of life that a Christian can expect as the Holy Spirit guides and empowers life. The minister who is committed to spiritual growth may begin with a self-evaluation in each of the nine qualities. Ask yourself how you are doing with love, joy, peace, patience, kindness, goodness, faithfulness, gentleness, self-control. Ask the question about each of these qualities in relation to yourself, your spouse, children, fellow church members, fellow ministers, and neighbors. The question may also be asked profitably in relation to the tasks you perform in your ministry. For example, how would you rate yourself in patience as you lead committees, councils, groups, and persons in their organizational work? Or, to what extent does joy show up in your preaching and faithfulness show up in guarding your study preparation for preaching?

Self-evaluation will provide a basis for setting some growth goals. One goal might be to reach the point in leadership relationships where you consistently look for solutions to unresolved problems or incomplete projects rather than heaping blame on yourself or others. Next-step goals may include building prayer for patience into your daily devotional life and a schedule for regularly reviewing the big picture and overall progress in ministry. This review will help to keep people and projects in the context of a grand design rather than to view the total worth of your ministry as hanging on one happening or the success of one project. This kind of action reveals that you are acting responsibly in managing the spiritual growth in your life.

Reserve Some Time for Managing Spiritual Growth
Personal responsibility demands that the minister block out some time daily for responding to personal spiritual needs. Personal

prayer and study retreats should be built into the calendar at regular intervals. They should be guarded as high priority commitments. Blocking out the time and being faithful in keeping it are the minister's responsibilities. No one else in the church or community will assume that responsibility for you.

The third section of this chapter will explore some spiritual exercises through which a Christian can grow. Busy ministers know that it takes discipline to manage one's life to be faithful to these spiritual disciplines.

Provide for regular checkups.—Preventive medicine has become standard in the medical profession. Regular checkups are encouraged. Many corporations require their executives to have periodic physical examinations. The corporation has a great investment in these executives and wants to reduce as much as possible the danger of their sudden loss through preventable sickness or death. Of greater importance is the fact that most persons really care about the health and well-being of their associates and friends and want to encourage them to stay well.

Regular checkups are as vital to spiritual growth as they are to physical health. Unhealthy thought patterns, personal habits, and attitudes can find their way unnoticed into our lives. They begin to drain us of spiritual vitality in much the same way that infections drain the body of physical vitality. Spiritual growth checkups can help us in the early detection stage of spiritual depletion.

Make a checklist of the qualities you desire to encourage in your life. Earlier it was suggested that you might use the qualities of the fruit of the Spirit as interpreted by Paul. If you follow this suggestion, list them in the left column of a sheet of paper. In the middle column write some notes about how you are doing in each of these qualities. Ask the Holy Spirit to bring to your consciousness the reality about love, joy, and peace in all the relationships of your life. In the third column of the page make some notes of actions you desire to take to help you grow in the expression of each of these qualities. Since this is a personal exercise, you can be totally honest in your self-evaluation and specific in the actions you propose to take for growth.

Set aside at least two or three hours at the beginning of each month for your spiritual checkup. Spend some of the time in devotional Bible reading and prayer. God will help you understand yourself better and diagnose more effectively in that environment.

Spiritual Growth Requires a Clear Focus on Personal Mission

Ministers who are uncertain about who they really are or why they are doing what they are doing are not likely candidates for healthy spiritual growth. The familiar one-word questions—who, why, what, where, when—call the growing minister to a continuing, honest, and personal search. Who am I? How have I become what I am? Why am I giving my life to serve God and these people? What am I to do as a called-out disciple of Christ? Where am I to serve him? In what places can God best use my life? When am I to change my place of service and my role in ministry?

There are no easy formulas to follow in finding answers to these questions. The beginning point must certainly be openness to the leadership of the Holy Spirit. In an honest-to-God attitude, with careful attention to God's Word and prayerful conversation with God, a minister can discover many of the answers to life's one-word questions. At least the minister need not be paralyzed into indecision or forced into making decisions frantically or haphazardly. The personal understanding of one's mission can be found by examining two sources of information. Spiritual growth requires the integration of these two sources of information in a way that clarifies personal mission and gives the push to becoming the person God had in mind.

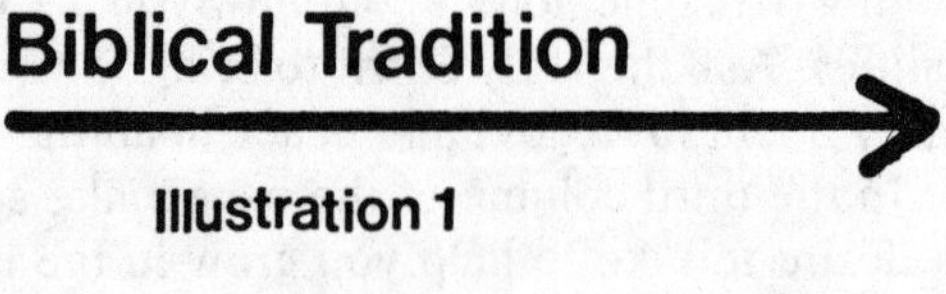

Biblical Tradition

→

Illustration 1

Personal Mission Is Clarified by Biblical Tradition
The spiritual peaks of the Hebrew people recorded in the Old Testament were in direct relation to their commitment to God.

Being the people of God in a world of idolatry was their calling, their privilege, and their hope. Awareness of their mission was stirred regularly as they observed the Passover meal and other celebrations. They focused on the victories of their ancestors who lived faithfully as the people of God. Out of the strength of their godly tradition, they were humble and confident.

When their consciousness of being the people of God grew dim, they took on the characteristics of their neighbors who did not honor God. They lived as though their mission was to become powerful through their own clever devices rather than through being the people of God and continuing in the will of God. Out of touch with their spiritual tradition, they became a people with no mission.

Jesus knew from whence he had come. He declared that he was one with the Father. This awareness caused him to reject the shortcuts to success offered by Satan, the nationalistic prejudices offered by the Sadducees, and the unredemptive judgment offered by the scribes and Pharisees. Knowing that he was the Son of God sent by the Father on a loving mission to mankind, Jesus would not be turned aside from the nature and purpose of his life on earth. He was of the Father, in the Father's world, and for the redemption of the people chosen by the Father. His mission was in the mind of God from the day of creation and would be until the final day of redemption. He would not be inconsistent with his Father.

Each follower of Jesus walks onto the line of biblical tradition that flows through Abraham, Isaac, Jacob, and the prophets and priests who faithfully revealed the truth of Jehovah God. The follower of Jesus is not free to start off on a new course. He is not free to create his mission apart from the directions given by biblical tradition. The who-am-I, why-am-I-here, and what-am-I-to-do questions are answered as we see God working with man in history. Our worship of God in awesome devotional experiences and faithful service grows out of this awareness.

Personal Mission Is Clarified by the Circumstances of Contemporary Life
If our devotional life only touches the biblical tradition, we may

Contemporary Life

Illustration 2

find ourselves out of touch with reality in the here and now. The second illustration calls our attention to the reality of the incarnation. Jesus was not simply the Son of God loving man and seeking man's redemption. He was the Son of God in human flesh walking the streets of Jerusalem, the shores of Galilee, and the slopes of Mt. Hermon. He did this at a particular time in history, a time when the world was moving from twilight to darkness socially, morally, and spiritually. Being filled with the Spirit, he was able to confront Satan, have patience with slow-learning disciples, forgive sinners, heal the sick and broken, and go through Gethsemane to death on a cross. The Spirit of God did not take Jesus away from the pains of life on earth at that time and place. Rather, the Spirit enabled Jesus to be the Son of God, to be harmonious with the eternal tradition, in a world that had come to be out of tune with God. It is evident that the mission was clear to Jesus because he remained faithful to the nature of God in the particular circumstances that characterized his time and place. His summary was: "The Son of Man is come [from the eternal God] to seek [in this time and place] and to save that which was lost" (Luke 19:10). He worked with the disciples to prepare them to continue seeking in their times and in their places those who are lost and to direct the lost ones to Jesus who can save them.

Ministers who grow spiritually will do so as they accept the Holy Spirit's revelation of what it means to be God's person in today's world. They will study and pray with the Bible in one hand and today's newspaper in the other. They will not complain because of the high demands of the biblical tradition or because of the high calling of God this tradition expresses. Nor will they complain because of the high demands of the times and places in which they are asked to serve. Instead they will grow in awareness of their mission in life as they nurture the dialogue between the eternal truth of the biblical tradition that sends them forth into the world. They will grapple with the challenge in how one lives effectively as God's kind of person in man's kind of world. We must not close the devotional closet so tightly that the aches and pains of living in a world like ours can't get to the prayer bench.

The dialogue in the third illustration brings the biblical tradition and contemporary life together into mission with a sharp focus. Spiritual growth requires this dialogue and is nurtured by it.

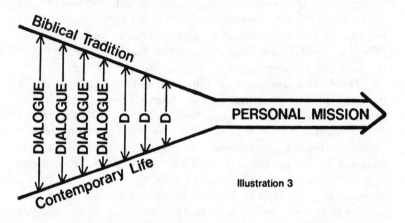

Illustration 3

Spiritual Growth Requires Maintaining Devotional Disciplines

A healthy devotional life requires discipline involving persistence, patience, time, and effort. Devotional gimmickry is not an effective approach to devotional health. Gimmickry in the devotional life leads from one fad to another in a search for spiritual growth. Often the more novel the devotional activity the more effective it is reputed to be in producing spiritual growth. The pastor who follows a friend's suggestion that the greatest way to a really successful devotional life involves praying from two to four in the morning may find himself pleased with his marathon effort in prayer but asleep while trying to prepare two sermons for next Sunday. For one person that prayer time may be ideal for rewarding devotional experiences; for another it will only be a gimmick for which he can congratulate himself.

Devotional snobbery is not an expression of devotional health. A familiar biblical account of devotional snobbery is found in a parable Jesus spoke. "Two men went up into the temple to pray; the one a Pharisee, and the other a publican. The Pharisee stood and prayed thus with himself, God, I thank thee, that I am not as other men are, extortioners, unjust, adulterers, or even as this publican. I fast twice in the week, I give tithes of all that I possess" (Luke 18:10-12). Jesus declared that an ashamed sinner who confessed his sin was justified before God more than a man who displayed devotional snobbery. No person is more holy because he performs certain religious routines. He is more holy only if he displays a broken and contrite heart and confidence in the love and power with which God approaches sinners.

Devotional legalism is not healthy either. Legalism in the devotional life implies that God is obligated by our practices to grant what we desire. A high-school student went by the church every morning on his way to school. A friend questioned him about his reasons for observing the pattern ritualistically. He responded by sharing his fear that God would no longer keep him safe and help him make good grades if he failed to go by the church and pray. God is obligated by his nature, not by our bargaining behavior. Persons who feel that they are able to obligate God usually judge the spiritual health of others on the basis of whether others conform to their devotional pattern. Like the Old Testament Hebrews, they feel that prosperity is a sure sign of rightness with God. The rich and powerful people Jesus denounced teach us it is not so.

Gimmickry, snobbery, and legalism are not as devastating to spiritual growth as is devotional starvation. Some ministers become so busy feeding others that they don't have time to personally feed on God's Word or be nurtured through prayer and meditation. Others become careless and unaware that spiritual malnutrition is gradually weakening them until they become victims of a trying circumstance that threatens to destroy their ministry. Like Samson they rise up to do battle with the enemy only to find that their strength is gone.

The healthy minister is aware that devotional starvation is a more dangerous potential than physical starvation, so he may find himself fasting in order to feast on the fellowship with God and the urgent ministry opportunities with which God surrounds him.

Devotional disciplines are intended for ordinary human beings in the midst of normal daily activities. They are not to be limited to the dramatic and challenging experiences of life such as church revival weeks or in decision-making experiences when a minister must decide whether to go to a new place of ministry or stay where he is. Devotional disciplines, maintained regularly, save us from having to cram with panic to be ready for some particular test in life. Maintaining regular devotional disciplines enables us to carry out our normal daily activities with confidence and strength rather than feeling that we must run away from the routines of life in order to be close to God.

It would be presumptuous to attempt to present all of the possible spiritual growth disciplines in a few pages. Volumes have been written without exhausting the possibilities. Personalities vary so much that one person's blessing is another person's burden. Therefore, the treatment of spiritual growth disciplines will be limited to some general categories like meditation, study, prayer, worship, and fasting. These disciplines are not clearly distinct from one another. They spill over and find their expressions in each other. The minister engaged in personal worship, caught up in exalting God in His worthiness, may be brought to worship through Bible study and then find himself praying and meditating.

The Discipline of Meditation

The Bible calls God's people to meditation, to focus the mind on the truth God reveals. It is tragic that the emergence of Eastern religions and their disciplines in our culture have caused some Christians to hesitate to speak about meditation. Transcendental meditation has been popularized because of a vacuum of teaching and training in the discipline of meditation among Western Christians. Richard J. Foster rebuked contemporary Christian leaders for their failure to teach and train persons in the discipline of meditation. "It is a sad commentary on the spiritual state of modern Christianity that meditation is a word so foreign to its ears. Meditation has always stood as a classical and central part of

Christian devotion, a crucial preparation for and adjunct to the work of prayer. No doubt part of the surge of interest in Eastern meditation is because the churches have abrogated the field."[3]

Our code words are *rush, talk, work, play, eat,* and *sleep.* The Bible calls us to meditate. Meditation is emptying the mind of code words in order to fill the mind with truth about the kingdom of God and his righteousness. Meditation is basking one's being in the warmth of the reality of God's presence and power in his world. The evidences of God's presence and power are all around us. The glory of God calls forth our meditation—our quiet, searching, submissive response to the reality of God in his world.

As you read the Bible, allowing its message to capture your mind, you will get captured with an impression of God's glory that you should stop and think about for a while. The remarks of Jesus about the lilies of the field or the birds of the air may cause you to recall the most beautiful field you ever walked through or the soaring eagle whose grace and power caused you to watch with awe. Stop your reading long enough to reflect on these reminders of the wonder of God. Close your eyes, and with your mind's help walk through that field again. Smell the flowers. Capture the colors with the camera of your mind. Feel the cool breeze, and watch it rustle the leaves and tall grass. Hum or sing:

> This is my Father's world,
> The birds their carols raise;
> The morning light, the lily white
> Declare their makers praise.
> This is my Father's world,
> He shines in all that's fair;
> In the rustling grass I hear him pass,
> He speaks to me ev'rywhere.[4]

Get out into the woods or high on a hill or mountainside, and let the beauty and power of nature remind you of truth about yourself. In that setting read Psalm 8 and other psalms, and celebrate your being as the exalted creation of God.

As a part of your preparation to lead a worship service, go into the empty worship center and let its silence give way to the voices of meditation. Look at the pews and, with your mind, seat people in them. Look at the persons who will be seated there when you lead the congregation in worship on Sunday. Move beyond the surface expressions with your gaze. Ask the Spirit of God to help you feel their feelings of joy or sorrow, anxiety or hope. Let them speak their feelings to you. In this meditation experience you will hear the people call out to you for help, and you will hear Paul's reminder that you can do all that is needed through the strength Christ offers you. Elizabeth Barrett Browning wrote a proverb in poetry that calls us to meditation.

> Earth's crammed with heaven,
> And every common bush afire with God;
> But only he who sees, takes off his shoes—
> The rest sit around it and pluck blackberries,
> and daub their natural faces unaware.[5]

For more specific suggestions of meditation experiences, see *Celebration of Discipline* by Richard Foster.[6] He provides exercises for "centering down" and meditating on creation and Scripture and the meditative use of imagination. *Creative Brooding* by Robert Raines provides useful printed meditations that stimulate the mind.[7] Wayne Oates can help you integrate silence with the demands and pressures made upon you every day through his book *Nurturing Silence in a Noisy Heart*.[8]

The Discipline of Study
Effective devotional study is the activity of examining one's life in relation to God and other persons with the aid of resources which stimulate thought. Study is analytical. Study asks questions like: What is the meaning in this for me? If I believe this, what do I do about it? How can I make this work in my life?

In devotional study the first resource is the Bible. Read it to be changed. In professional study you will read the Bible to gather information that can be organized and presented to persons in a variety of settings and for a variety of purposes. Devotional study is more narrow in focus. Read with analytical questions in mind. There is room for change and need for change in your personal life. Let the Bible call attention to problems and potential. Let it judge you, instruct you, affirm you, and guide you.

There are many ways to organize devotional Bible study. Getting to it on a regular basis with an unhurried mind is the greatest challenge. I am presently finding personal profit in beginning my day with reading five psalms, two chapters of Proverbs, two Old Testament chapters, and one New Testament chapter. Some may find this approach too fragmented. I have found it useful as a devotional study approach. Reading larger portions, even one or more books of the Bible, may be the approach that satisfies your devotional study needs.

Structure a private study retreat for a day or two. Get away from home or the office where you can put in ten or twelve study hours a day. Combine devotional Bible study and inspiring experiences with nature. Read large portions of the Scripture to catch the panorama of God's movement with his creation, and place yourself in the picture.

Combine your study of the Bible with study of some of the devotional classics. There are many excellent resources available in your library, the church library, or public libraries. Ministers should own some devotional classics, so they may read them again and again. An excellent guide to the use of devotional classics is found in *Seekers after a Mature Faith*.[9] The author introduces classics provided by Christians from the past and the present. Most familiar among them are Augustine's *Confessions*, Thomas a Kempis' *The Imitation of Christ*, Brother Lawrence's *The Practice of the Presence of God*, John Bunyan's *The Pilgrim's Progress*, and Bonhoeffer's *Letters and Papers from Prison* and *The Cost of Discipleship*.

The Discipline of Prayer

As in the case of a minister's Bible study, there is the danger that prayer will become a job-related activity rather than a personal experience in spiritual growth. Supporting others through prayer or enriching one's work of personal witnessing, preaching, singing, or teaching through prayer are not as important to the minister as growing one's life through personal prayer fellowship with the heavenly Father.

Take time to pray. If we don't take time to pray, we will fill the little bit of time with our words. Since prayer is at least as much listening as it is talking, we need time to listen as the Spirit of God speaks, sometimes comfortingly and sometimes disquietingly, to our hearts. The time for prayer and the forms of prayer that are most effective vary for different persons. Hinson said about the forms of prayer that which can also be said about the times: "What matters, of course, is not the forms but prayer itself, namely conversation, communion, or communication between ourselves as personal beings and God, the heavenly Father, as the ultimate personal reality in the universe. What matters further is how this engagement with God carries over into all dimensions of our personal lives and our society."[10]

We need to relearn the reasons for prayer and the rudiments of prayer from a study of the Gospels, then organize the use of our days to guarantee that we preserve time for prayer. Those who have mastered this discipline testify that the satisfactions of a disciplined prayer life cause them to desire to spend more and more time in prayer. Fellowship with the heavenly Father really is rewarding once you have been with him enough to cease being afraid or feeling awkward in his presence.

The Discipline of Worship

Devotional worship occurs when one person prostrates his life before God the Creator and aligns himself as a willing and joyous servant of God. Worship can occur when a person is alone, when two or three are gathered together in Jesus' name, or when a large congregation of persons is one in God's common purpose for them. Regardless of the setting, worship is essentially personal. It is a human response in awareness of the initiative of God to save man from self-destruction.

As an aide to personal worship, look at the hymns of worship, hymns that exalt God and express adoration toward God. Get alone on your knees and read the hymn as your statement of adoration. Read them together or sing them as a family worshiping God. In addition to the hymns, lead your family in reading psalms of adoration, like Psalms 19, 24, 100, and 103. Write your own words of adoration in which you describe God in relation to your life. Read these words aloud to God. Ask the other members of your family to write their words of adoration and provide a time when family members may share these with each other as they express them aloud to God.

Worship that begins in adoration moves naturally to praising God, confessing our sins to God, interceding for others, petitioning God for our daily bread and other needs, and committing ourselves to God for the work he needs us to do. Out of that grows the motivation for ministry to others in Jesus' name which is the social dimension of worship. The cup of water given lovingly in Jesus' name is a continuation of the expression that began in the adoration of God by one of his reverent children.

The Discipline of Fasting

Fasting may be the most misunderstood and abused devotional discipline. Jesus cautioned his contemporaries about making a public display or a fetish of fasting. In our day most Christians react by going to the opposite extreme and shunning any consideration of fasting as a devotional discipline. A Christian's interest in fasting grows out of a concern that is greater than dieting for weight loss. It grows out of the awareness of numerous biblical examples where fasting related to spiritual growth and spiritual victory. Moses, Elijah, Daniel, and many other spiritual leaders of the Old Testament fasted. Jesus fasted, as did John's disciples, Cornelius, and Paul. And Jesus instructed his disciples in proper attitudes for one who fasts (see Matt. 6:16-18).

"Throughout Scripture fasting refers to abstaining from food for spiritual purposes."[11] Fasting results from a conscious commitment to abstaining from normal eating patterns for a period of time in order to invest one's total time and energy resources in pursuing a spiritual objective. The spiritual objective may be to meet a specific ministry need, to concentrate total attention on God's mission for one's life.

Fasting should always center on God; worship and fasting are healthy partners. Healthy fasting helps us to better understand the things that control us and to keep a balance in life. If the worshiper refrains from calling attention to the fast, as Jesus instructed in Matthew 6:16-18, and goes about the regular routines of life, the discipline can sharpen his awareness of God and of self. Fasting that is not designed to impress others can enhance spiritual growth and that without imposing any danger to physical health.

Some ministers are working hard to get their churches to experience growth and feeling frustrated, perhaps defeated, in the efforts. A minister can influence church growth but not control it. The one area where you as a minister hold the reigns is the area of spiritual growth. Not only are you able to determine whether you grow or not, but you are also the only one who can be responsible for your growth. And the extra reward is that your spiritual growth will be a model for others in the church. Your celebration of growth will bring celebration in the lives of others who share the blessing.

1. Richard J. Foster, *Celebration of Discipline* (San Francisco: Harper & Row, 1978), p. 1.
2. Ernest E. Mosley, *Priorities in Ministry* (Nashville: Convention, 1978).
3. Foster, p. 14.
4. From "This Is My Father's World" by Maltbie D. Babcock.
5. From *Aurora Leigh* by Elizabeth Barrett Browning.
6. Foster, pages 24-29.
7. Robert Raines, *Creative Brooding* (New York: Macmillan, 1966).
8. Wayne E. Oates, *Nurturing Silence in a Noisy Heart* (Garden City, New York: Doubleday, 1979).
9. Glenn Hinson and Wayne E. Oates, *Seekers After a Mature Faith* (Nashville: Broadman, 1968).
10. E. Glenn Hinson, *The Reaffirmation of Prayer* (Broadman: Nashville, 1979), p. 10.
11. Foster, p. 42.